Flea *Flicker*

Essays on Family, Marriage, and Youth Sports

TIM HIRSCHBECK

*TO KARY,
HAPPY NEW BABY!
ALL THE BEST ON THE
NEW ADDITION TO YOUR
FAMILY*

ISBN: 1453841784
ISBN-13: 9781453841785

For Tricia, Molly, and Zac

Contents

Acknowledgements i

Introduction iii

I Believe 1

Mr. Phelps 5

70% 9

Outsourcing 13

Sister Mary Brass Knuckles.............................. 17

The Bad Kid... 21

Someday You'll Thank Me For This.................... 23

The Enemy.. 29

Accoutrements 33

The Boy Behind the Mask 37

Pay Me My Money Down 41

1972.. 47

My Boy 51

Mrs. Menas.. 55

My Big Blunder 61

Fumblebum.. 65

Copenhagen... 69

Bobby.. 73

The Seven Demandments 79

The Oath... 83

The Price You Pay 87

CETA 91

Treasure Hunt 95

The Boy With One Name....................................101

Matt and Andy 105

Future Ghosts and Mr. Hair Gel 109

The Assassin 113

The Summer of Stunk..117

Hooks..121

The Food Chain 125

The Battle of Diminished Expectations.................129

You Might Be a Helicopter Parent If... 133

Choosing Teams 137

Psycho Stories...143

The Pizza Mom 147

The T-Ball Calls 151

Everybody Makes the Team 155

Participation Trophies 159

Flea Flicker..165

Specialization 169

Stupid 175

I'm Losing You...179

Our Work Here Is Done 181

Walk Away Little Girl...185

Acknowledgements

Thanks to the players, coaches, parents, and school district partners that have kept KidsPlay rolling for the past twenty years. I owe a significant part of my happiness to my job and I owe my job to you.

The bulk of my professional education has come from watching great coaches and teachers at work. I'm indebted to all those who have shared their guidance, wisdom, and sense of humor with me. Special thanks to Chris Hirschbeck, Mike Czerwinski, Ann Mischler, Bob Vorburger, Jeff Scott, John Rojek, Jerry Miller, Pete and Sandy Allen, Joe Gentile, Amanda Veazie, Phil DiNunzio, Todd Marquardt, Ken Voght, Tim Grant, Matt Leary, Patricia Hilbert, Geza Csonka, Kevin Caputi, Marilyn Sozanski, Betty Philage, Scott Zwink, Jack Flatau, and all the great teachers in the Kenmore-Tonawanda School District who have welcomed my son and daughter into their classroom.

I'm lucky to count an editor and an author among my good friends. One thousand greasy breakfasts cannot begin to thank Mick and Mary Cochrane for revealing the secrets of the enigmatic semicolon and giving me invaluable help in editing this book.

Thanks to Mike, Bill, Judy, and Chris for taking me under their wing and bringing more warmth and fun into my childhood.

If you hold this book up to your ear in a quiet room, you can hear my mom's voice on every page. I think about her every day and carry her memory in my heart forever.

All my love and gratitude to Tricia, Molly and Zac for bringing immeasurable light and love into my life.

Introduction

There's not a lot that distinguishes me from the rest of the guys in my neighborhood. Like most 46-year-old men, my hair follicles and brain cells are evaporating at alarming rates. I mow the lawn, plow the snow, and lend constant care and comfort to our dog, Lily. In return for completing those three jobs to my wife's satisfaction, I'm given possession of any and all remote controls in our home.

Perhaps the only unique thing about me is that I've spent the better part of 32 years teaching kids to play sports. A conservative guess is that I've worked with at least 85,000 young athletes, 2,000 parent volunteers, and 260 paid staff over the years. When it comes to running youth sports leagues that are fun, fair, and challenging for all players, I'd like to think I know a little more than the next guy. If you stick around long enough, it's impossible not to learn a few things along the way.

My education has not always come easily. On matters related to coaching young athletes and raising a child of my own, I arrived to the party way too early. I was barely 14 years old the first time I stepped out onto a field to coach a group of young soccer players, a boy barking orders at slightly younger boys. Just a few weeks before my wife and I found ourselves screaming and hyperventilating in a hospital delivery room for the first time, I had blown out 22 candles on a birthday cake. Under ideal circumstances, a 14-year-old should never be left in charge of a dozen impressionable soccer players and a 22-year-old should never be allowed to be fruitful and multiply.

My first several years of being a coach and a dad were filled with joy and self-loathing. The kids that I coached and the beautiful little girl I came home to every night brought immeasurable love and a strong sense of purpose into my life. Yet there was always a nagging sense that I was failing my kids. Youth and inexperience chiseled an extensive list of character flaws into my psyche. In my mind, laziness, narcissism, and a general sense of inferiority all seemed to be engaged in a daily competition to decide my greatest defect as a parent and a coach.

What do you do when you are pretty sure that you stink at handling life's greatest responsibilities? At first, I pretended that I was both a fine coach and strong candidate for Father of the Year. When living a life of make-believe didn't work, I ran away from my responsibilities, drank lots of beer, and blamed everything on my wife.

The thing that snapped me back to the real world and forced me to honestly assess my contributions to my work and family was the simple act of writing. When I argued with my wife or tried to justify my mistakes to those who loved me, I could convince my harshest critic that the sky was purple and I was a great guy. There was something about writing that cut through all the crap. Assembling semi-coherent sentences on my computer screen forced me to confront some unpleasant truths about myself and on some occasions, helped to reaffirm some of the good decisions I felt I was making as a parent and a coach.

Twenty years ago, I began to share some of my writing with other parents and coaches. The first essay I ever sent out to a friend included a note that would have made an appropriate attachment to every piece of writing I published thereafter: Hope you don't think I'm trying to tell you what to do, I wrote to my friend; just wanted to share my views in the hopes it might help you clarify your own.

While I'm on the subject of clarifying one's views, there are a few notes I feel obliged to share that might make the process of reading this book more enjoyable and less confusing.

First, my wife and kids have graciously allowed me to use their real names and life experiences in this book. The names of all other characters have been changed to protect the innocent, the guilty, and the future safety of the author.

Surprisingly, the most challenging task associated with writing this book was figuring out how to sort and present these essays. In the end, I've chosen to assemble these stories much in the same way that I would a collection of photographs that I gave to a good friend. Each essay represents a particular place and time, showing what I and members of my family looked like in the collective fleeting moments that make up our shared history. Because these essays are not grouped chronologically, my son might be 15 years old on page 38 and seven years old on page 112. My apologies in advance if that time warp makes your head explode.

Finally, be forewarned that there are no expert opinions or definitive answers in the pages ahead, for it has been my experience that there aren't many indisputable facts associated with being a dad or a coach. The suggestion that there is only one way to run a successful youth sports program makes as much sense as the suggestion that there is only one way to raise a great kid.

In many respects, being a good coach or parent is a natural and intuitive thing. One of the pleasures of working with children is that each day brings a new set of unexpected challenges. Strong coaches and parents must rely on intuition, common sense, and the ability to remain calm when surrounded by chaos. I can't teach you to be more intuitive or judicious, but I can tell you what I've learned coaching and raising kids over the past 32 years in the hope that you will benefit from my experience.

This is what I've learned.

Kenmore, New York
July 18th, 2010

I Believe

In 1991, my wife and I and a bunch of our friends started a company called KidsPlay. Over the past two decades, our coaches have taught over 75,000 young athletes to honor the game by playing hard, playing fair, and playing together. Hopefully, we've brought a significant amount of goodwill into our community and maybe even changed the way that some parents and players view youth sports.

When I started writing this book, I had to decide how much mention our little company would get in these pages. The answer that makes the most sense to me is to refrain from mentioning KidsPlay as much as possible for two reasons. First, I don't want the book to wind up sounding like a thinly veiled vehicle to promote our company. Second, I feel barely qualified to write about being a husband, father, and coach, but grossly unqualified to write about owning a successful small business. The only unique piece of advice I could give you about starting your own business is to find my wife and convince her to marry you.

Most of the small-business owners I've met over the years mark the start of their company by the day they earned their first dollar or filed their papers at County Hall. I have no memory of either event. For me, KidsPlay started on a sunny Saturday morning in May 1991. My lovely wife was up in bed reading the newspaper and soaking in the breeze that filtered through the curtains. I was lying next to her, eating a bowl of cereal and reading a book. Our five-year-old daughter was across the hall in her bedroom having a picnic with an assortment of Barbies and stuffed animals.

On the surface, we looked like the perfect picture of the happy American family. Below the surface, there was a significant amount of stress in our house. Tricia had recently started a new job at a local hospital and while she loved the job, she was concerned that she was on shaky ground with her new employers. She was six months pregnant at the time and perpetually queasy. The number of times that she threw up each day was roughly equal to the number of hours of sleep she got each night.

I was putting in a lot of hours at my job and enjoying my work less and less. I was sick and tired of battling my supervisors whenever I wanted to spend a few bucks on the kids in my programs. There always seemed to be enough money in the budget to send the VP of operations to a seminar in Washington, DC, but there never seemed to be enough money to replace broken equipment or pay my staff a decent wage.

Our greatest concern was the little girl across the hall. Our new work schedules had forced us to put Molly in daycare for a few hours in the afternoon. It was a nice place with good teachers, but neither of us was happy with the situation. Molly had started to develop a continuous string of ear and sinus infections that she'd trade back and forth with the other kids in her class. Tricia and I hated the sad, indifferent look on our daughter's face when we dropped her off at the center. Daycare can serve as a lifesaver for some families, but it wasn't working for us.

My heart racing furiously, I put my book down on the bedside table, turned to my wife, and blurted out a secret that had been swirling around in my head for a few months, "I don't want to do this anymore, Tricia."

"What do you mean?" She looked surprised, concerned, and slightly amused all at the same time.

"Work," I said. "I don't think I can work at that place anymore." Frustration and anger spilled out of me. I don't think I realized how much I hated my job until I said the words out loud. Working for people that I didn't respect was eating me up.

Tricia patiently listened to me rant for at least 30 minutes. At the end of my tirade, I summed things up:

I loved my wife and our little girl with all my heart.

I couldn't wait to bring our new baby into the world.

I was unhappy with everything else in my life.

"So what do you want to do?" she asked. It was a reasonable question. If I was going to leave my job, there had to be some sort of plan, right? Any guy in his right mind wasn't going to quit his job without knowing what comes next.

I had no plan. My strengths were spewing ideas and complaining about my current job; performing research and crafting any kind of operational strategy were my obvious weaknesses. I told Tricia that I was interested in starting my own business and I wanted to continue working with kids. Maybe I could open a sporting goods store that catered exclusively to children. Or perhaps I could sell uniforms and equipment to sports teams. I had some very specific ideas about how youth sports leagues should be run; maybe I could open my own gym.

Let's pause for a second to look at things from Tricia's point of view. You're six months pregnant and throwing up two to three times a day. Nine months ago, you moved into your first house and began paying a mortgage for the first time. You've got a beautiful five-year-old little girl who is due to start kindergarten next year. Four weeks ago, you started a demanding new job. Life is filled with lots of love, but it's also filled with car payments, utility bills, and a dwindling savings account. And now your goofy husband is telling you that he wants to quit his job, but he's not exactly sure what he wants to do next.

She had every right to suggest that it wasn't a good idea to quit my job until I found another one. Hell, she had every right to slap me upside the head and tell me to haul my butt back to work immediately. Instead, Tricia looked at me with those beautiful green eyes and said, "Well, whatever you decide to do, I know you'll do great."

It was the greatest gift of love and faith that anyone has ever given to me.

KidsPlay was an enormous risk. Back in 1991, teaching kids to play sports without scoreboards and standings was a pretty radical concept. Right up to the day we opened our doors, I wasn't sure that people would come. But they did. What started as me and a friend teaching 80 kids to play soccer quickly turned into over 30 coaches and hundreds of parent coaches teaching 6,000 young athletes every year. All of the good things that KidsPlay has brought into our community trace their way back to my lovely wife. If she had said anything different on that sunny Saturday morning 20 years ago, KidsPlay would have never happened.

Sometimes I wonder what the world would be like if there were more people like my wife in it, people who have an open heart and the courage to look in the eyes of the one they love and say, "Whatever you decide to do, I know you'll do great." Tricia's leap of faith has sustained me for the past two decades. How much more light and love would there be in the world if more people were willing to take a similar leap?

Good coaches have a variety of tools and skills at their command. The best coaches I have met in my travels are part teacher, part motivator, part disciplinarian, part minister, part strategist, part counselor, part comedian, and part confidante. Yet I think the most important tool that coaches have in their toolbox is the ability to look one of their players in the eye and say four very powerful words:

I believe in you.

Mr. Phelps

Though I grew up in a home without a father, I had three brothers who took turns assuming the role of a father figure in my life. Collectively, they made sure I didn't miss out on the traditional things that fathers do with their sons. The major bonus was that my brothers were a lot cooler than the other dads in our neighborhood. All the other dads I knew listened to the Bee Gees and had 9-to-5 jobs. My brothers had hair down to their shoulders and maintained regular contact with local law enforcement. All of my friends had Ozzie Nelson for a dad. I had Keith Richards, Robert Plant, and Al "The Mad Hungarian" Hrabosky.

The first thing that truly connected me to my brothers was baseball. When I was seven years old, there was a nameless game that I'd play almost every day with the three kings. It involved me standing between two elm trees out in front of our house while my brothers stood with a bat and ball 10 yards away. The object of the game was for one of my brothers to hit a ball past me and between the two elm trees. The scoring system was simple: I received zero points for every ball I fielded cleanly, and my brothers received an automatic win if they could make me quit. For me, that nameless game was all about respect. My goal was to make a catch so spectacular that it would make one of my brothers begrudgingly mutter something like "Good catch" or "Big deal, you don't suck. Do you want a medal or something?" I happily dove on cement and crashed into trees in order to hear one of the kings say I didn't suck.

In my town, a boy had to be at least eight years old in order to play Little League baseball. I started playing when I was six not because I was the next Mickey Mantle, but because one of my brothers falsified my birth date on my registration form. At age six, the ethical implications of falsifying a birth date didn't matter to me. I was just proud that one of my brothers thought I was good enough to play with the big kids.

And it turned out that I was good enough. Despite the fact that I was a year or two younger than every one else, I was my team's starting shortstop. I still struck out more than I got on base, but I was a fielding virtuoso. All those years of having baseballs hit at my head in front of our house had served me well.

The only downside to playing Little League baseball was my coach. In the two years that I played for him, Mr. Phelps did the same thing at every single practice. For the first 30 minutes of each practice, Mr. Phelps would stick us out in the field and hit us grounders and pop-ups. If we missed the ball, he'd offer encouraging words of inspiration like "What the hell was that?" or "you look like an idiot out there!"

The remaining 60 minutes of each practice saw Mr. Phelps rotate every player in to take 10 swings at the ball while he pitched to us. If we missed a few pitches, Mr. Phelps always offered the same piece of incisive instruction: "Watch the ball!" If we missed more than a few pitches, it was always "Don't be afraid of the ball!" or "You're swinging like a fairy!"

He was short-tempered, ignorant, and prone to spewing profanity when provoked, but dealing with Coach Phelps was a necessary evil that allowed me to play a game that I loved.

By the time I was eight years old, it felt like I was on top of the Little League world. Not only was I finally old enough to legally play Little League ball, but with two years of illegal experience under my belt, I was one of the best players on our team. Dreams of batting cleanup and being named team captain floated around in my head. As our team started practicing that year, my only concern was that a couple of my friends were in danger of being cut from the team.

It's two weeks before the start of the season and Mr. Phelps gathers all of us together under a big old oak tree next to the baseball diamond where we practiced. My stomach is churning with equal parts excitement and dread. Will I be named captain? Will any of my buddies be cut from the team?

Mr. Phelps gets right to the point. "None of you really stood out from the rest this season, so I've decided to make cuts in a different way." He holds up an empty coffee can and says, "I've written down all of your names on a piece of paper. The first four names that I pick out of the can will be cut from the team."

I'm stunned. Is this some sort of joke? None of us stood out from the rest? There were at least four kids on the team who hadn't gotten a hit during three weeks of tryouts. Carl Butterson and Tommy Kane threw like my grandmother who, at the time, was residing in a long-term care facility up by Lake Ontario. At least half a dozen kids in the group deserved to be cut, it was just a question of who stunk less than the others.

It feels like I've been placed in the middle of one of those R-rated war movies. Sixteen of us are gathered in a circle. Our eyes are darting back and forth between the rest of our teammates and that stupid coffee can in Mr. Phelps's hand. All of our hard work in the first three weeks of practice now is reduced to a game of Russian roulette. Who will be playing baseball this summer and who will get his head blown off?

Mr. Phelps reaches into the can and pulls out a white slip of paper. He looks around at the group and announces the name on the slip, "Carl Butterson."

No big shock. Carl Butterson is a fat kid who can't hit, hides Tootsie Rolls in his glove, and has no interest in playing baseball. If I were coach, he would have been my first cut. Now I'm starting to think that maybe this whole picking names out of a coffee can thing is some sort of scam. Maybe Mr. Phelps has a heart after all. Maybe he knows who he wants to cut, but he thinks it's better for guys like Carl to believe that they didn't make the team because their name got drawn out of a can, not because they stink at baseball.

Carl doesn't appear to be too upset about being cut as he gathers his mitt and walks away from the group. Mr. Phelps draws the next slip of paper and sighs heavily before announcing the next name. "Mark Heller." Holy crap. No one on the team believes what he just heard. Mark Heller is not only our best hitter, but he's the only guy on the team who can play catcher. It's clear that this isn't a scam. Everyone's name is in that coffee can and any of us could be cut. My head is spinning and the only thing I can think is, please, please, please don't let Mr. Phelps pick my name.

I look over at Mark. He's always been a big, strong kid. Now he's putting his glove over his face and tears are welling up in his eyes. Carl Butterson was happy to stroll off into the sunset and eat an entire bag of Twizzlers, but Mark Heller refuses to leave. He sits cross-legged against a tree, glove over his face, tears dripping off of his chin.

Mr. Phelps draws a third slip of paper out of the can and lets out another heavy sigh. The next name he announces is mine.

I have no recollection of how I left the field. My next memory is of running down the street to our house, my glove on my hand, trying to see through the tears in my eyes. The three kings had taught me that crying was for girls and wimps, and I had become skilled at holding in my emotions. I wanted to be a big guy and hold back the tears but it was no use. I was bawling.

Two of the kings and my mom were home when I burst through the door and ran up to my room. I tried to tell them what had happened but I was sobbing so hard that I couldn't speak. That warm spring night in 1972 was the only time in my life that I have been inconsolable. I couldn't talk and I could barely see through my tears. All I could do was cry.

The following day, two coaches called our house to ask if I would play on their teams. I was angry, hurt, and too busy wallowing in self-pity to play baseball for a new coach. Mr. Phelps's game of Russian roulette had not only stomped all over my love for baseball, he took away the only thing that earned me the respect and admiration of my brothers.

Ten years passed before I played organized baseball again.

70%

You won't read a lot of statistical data in this book, but here's one statistic that I hope will echo in your head through to the final chapter: according to the National Alliance for Youth Sports (NAYS), roughly 70 percent of kids quit playing league sports by the age of 13 and never play again. In other words, for every 10 five-year-olds playing mighty mite hockey, T-ball, or micro-soccer in your community today, only three will still be participating in any type of organized sports league eight years from now.

Imagine if that same shameful statistic were applied to our children's scholastic education. What would happen if over 70 percent of our children dropped out of school by the time they reached the seventh grade?

A Nation Of Dropouts! would be the top story in the 24-hour news cycle. Every parent, teacher, administrator, and politician in the United States would be charged with scrutinizing the way we teach our children about reading, writing, and arithmetic. Millions of parents would be picketing their local school board meetings and demanding immediate action be taken to slow the rate of attrition. The Oval Office and Congress would be proposing radical structural changes to our educational system designed to keep students in school longer. We wouldn't rest until we had repaired the problem.

It is understood that getting good grades in school is far more important than playing third base for the Delaware Donuts White Sox. In addition to preparing a child for their eventual entry into the workplace, a child's scholastic education trains them to solve problems, communicate effectively, and explore new frontiers. A great schoolteacher can inspire a student to follow their life's passion. When your kid applies for a job someday, his or her future employer won't be interested in how many goals they scored in their first season of travel soccer.

It would be foolish to suggest that a child's physical education is just as significant as their scholastic education. However, it would be just as foolish to suggest that physical education is insignificant.

Exercise fosters learning. A strong physical education curriculum teaches children how to eat, exercise, and play during their formative years. In addition to preparing a child for their eventual entry into the workplace, a child's physical education trains them to solve problems, communicate effectively, and explore new frontiers. A great coach can inspire players to follow their passion. (Is it just me or does this sound familiar?) And let's acknowledge a sacred parental secret that we like to hide from our children: when your kid applies for a job someday, his or her future employer won't be particularly interested in their fourth grade test scores.

Sadly, the days of children receiving their physical education in school via daily physical education classes and recess are long gone. According to the 2006 Shape of the Nation study, jointly conducted by the American Heart Association and the National Association for Sport and Physical Education, the percentage of students who attend a daily physical education class dropped from 42 percent in 1991 to 28 percent in 2003.

As daily physical education withers away, over 41 million kids currently participate in extracurricular youth sports like soccer, baseball, and football. Today's child is more likely to receive their physical education through organized youth sports leagues than games of tag or kickball in gym class. Gradually, a new template has been created for teaching children about sports, physical fitness, and health.

Is the new template working? Has the transition from daily physical education to private organized sports leagues created a nation of stronger, healthier children?

It appears as though we are failing miserably. According to the Centers for Disease Control, the number of children considered to be overweight has tripled since 1980. Over 16 percent of children ages six to 19 are currently overweight. Increased numbers of obese and overweight children are associated with an increased risk of diabetes, high blood pressure, high cholesterol, asthma, and joint problems. CDC data also notes that an increasing number of high school students use unhealthy methods to lose or maintain weight. A nationwide survey found that during the 30 days preceding the survey, 12.3 percent of students went without eating for 24 hours or more; 4.5 percent had vomited or taken laxatives in order to lose weight; and 6.3 percent had taken diet pills, powders, or liquids without a doctor's advice (no more statistics for the rest of the book, I promise).

If over 41 million children currently participate in youth sports leagues in the United States, why are kids considerably less healthy than they were 20 years ago?

There are several answers to that question and some have nothing to do with youth sports. Greater access to video games, computers, and other forms of technology increases the likelihood that children live a more sedentary lifestyle. Because most children are now driven or bused to school and other extracurricular activities, they do less walking and running. Today's families are smaller, which means children have fewer playmates at home.

That said, some measure of responsibility for today's lack of health and fitness in children can be traced to current models of youth sports leagues. Where physical education in school is inclusive to all students, today's youth sports leagues are largely exclusive activities. If parents do not have the money to pay league fees, their children cannot play. If parents cannot pay for uniforms or equipment, their children cannot play. If parents are unable to transport their children to practices and games, their children cannot—well, you get the picture.

Where physical education in school tends to be focused on fun, fitness, and fair play, most youth sports leagues are focused on competition. A seven-year-old who demonstrates strong skills, coordination and athletic ability is embraced with a river of reward, recognition and opportunity. A 7-year-old who lacks the ability to help the team compete is directed toward a seat on the bench.

Without any deliberate malice on their part, most youth leagues have constructed a wall between the haves and the have-nots. The new template makes physical education accessible to physically gifted children who are born to affluent parents with flexible schedules. Those who are not born into that subset of the population must figure out how to climb over the wall if they want to play ball.

One unfortunate lesson I've learned over the years is that in matters related to youth sports leagues, very few of us are interested in looking at the big picture. If our kids have a decent coach and their team wins some games, we're content to ignore the rest of the world. If I had a nickel for every time a parent or coach approached me and expressed concerns about the fact that roughly 70 percent of our nation's children quit playing all organized sports by the time they reach middle school, I wouldn't have a single nickel.

More than anything else, it is the inability to look at the big picture that prevents us from solving the problems that plague so many youth sports leagues. Until we start to look beyond our kids, our team, and our town, young athletes will continue to drop out of youth sports leagues in staggering numbers. If you enjoy watching your sons or daughters play sports, cherish the moments now because if they are like most kids, they won't be playing sports for very long.

Outsourcing

When my wife and I found out that we were expecting our first baby, the news filled us with immeasurable joy and fear. In our hearts, we knew that we could be great parents. In our heads, we were convinced that as a result of our poor parenting skills, our child would become infamous for killing a series of convenience store owners across the upper Midwest.

I think most prospective parents go through those conflicting emotions. Part of us wants to believe that we have the raw skills to gain induction into the Parenting Hall of Fame, and part of us recognizes that if we aren't careful, we can really screw up our kid's life.

When Tricia and I brought Molly home from the hospital, life was suddenly filled with a new set of questions and dilemmas. Should we let her cry if she won't go to sleep? How do you care for that purple rash under her chin? On those days when our own common sense failed us, we sought guidance from the human encyclopedia of all good parenting advice: my mom.

Things have worked out pretty well so far. To date, Molly hasn't killed a convenience store clerk—at least not yet.

When my friend and his wife found out that they were expecting their first child, they went out and bought books—lots and lots of books. Thumbing through every parenting guide ever written by T. Barry Brazelton seemed to give them comfort. For them, being a good parent was sort of like getting a good score on the SAT. If they studied the course curriculum long and hard enough, they were ready to pass the parenting test.

The problem with that line of thinking is that there isn't one standard parenting test. There are dozens of tests every day. If your nose is constantly stuck in a T. Barry Brazelton book, it tends to complicate, not clarify, the process of raising a child.

Over the past few years, I've grown to believe that there are more parents using a manual to raise their kids than using their own common sense. In support of this belief, I offer you Booty Camp.

Yesterday, I was thumbing through a recent issue of *People* magazine at my doctor's office when I stumbled upon an article that leads me to believe that we might be on the brink of the end of Western Civilization. No, I'm not talking about Sandra Bullock's marriage to a bike mechanic sporting what seems like 66 tattoos. The article in question is right there on page 79 next to a photo of a woman with a pink t-shirt that reads "BOOTY CAMP." The title of the article reads "When Parents Outsource."

According to the article, there is a growing trend in the United States of parents paying large sums of cash to young entrepreneurs who are willing to perform tasks traditionally left to moms and dads.

Meet Wendy Sweeney, a 35-year-old pediatric nurse from Hanover Park, Illinois, and the woman wearing the aforementioned "BOOTY CAMP" shirt. For $200, Miss Wendy will come to your home for five one-hour sessions and potty train your child for you.

You say your daughter won't stop sucking her thumb? Call Shari Green, a.k.a. "The Thumb Lady," who guarantees that your child will kick the habit in five sessions or she'll refund your $450 fee.

For a mere $200 an hour, Lynda White, an etiquette specialist from Colony, Texas, will come to your house and teach your son to keep his elbows off the table and chew with his mouth closed.

Here's my favorite. Since 2001, Aresh Mohrit, the owner of a company called High 5 and a self-described "bike tutor," has taught over 1,800 children to ride their bikes. In return for a fee of $60 per hour, Mohrit unburdens parents from the hassles of attaching training wheels and running behind their child's bike with their hand clenched to the back of the seat.

Of course, the Bike Tutor also unburdens parents from seeing the joy on their child's face when their wheels stop wobbling and they can ride a bike for the very first time.

Therein lies the thing that troubles me about outsourcing parental responsibilities. Somewhere over the course of the past 20 years, we've come to believe that raising kids is best left to the "experts." If our daughter wants to date boys at age 10, we're more likely to call Dr. Laura than our mom. If we're unsure that we have the patience and wisdom needed to potty train our son, we send them to Booty Camp instead of using our own common sense. Has there ever been a generation of parents that were so insecure in their abilities to make the right decisions for their kids?

Ten years ago, my son wanted to learn how to catch a football. At the time, there were at least 10,000 people in the United States who were more qualified than me to teach him. However, Zac didn't want Bill Parcells to teach him to play football. He wanted his dad.

My sense is that most kids are like Zac. While adults seem fixated on qualifications and expertise, children are more interested in spending time with someone they love. Looking back, was it more important that the person who potty trained you was a pediatric nurse or your mom?

As parents, I think we need to play close attention to the ratio of free play vs. the amount of technical instruction that our children receive. I might be able to do a better job of teaching your four-year-old son to throw and catch a baseball, but wouldn't it be more fun if you taught him instead?

It works like this:

> *You throw a baseball to your son, he misses it.*
> *You throw the ball again, he misses.*
> *He asks you what your favorite TV show is. You say SportsCenter.*
> *You ask him what show is his favorite. He says SportsCenter*
> *and Sponge Bob.*
> *You throw the ball, he misses.*
> *You show him how to catch with two hands.*
> *He asks if you like Sponge Bob; you tell him you think it's a pretty*
> *funny show.*

You throw the ball, he catches it.
You tell him that was a great catch; he's beaming because he
caught the ball.
And because his dad is proud of him.

I'd like to think that I'm a pretty good coach, but when it comes to playing catch with your child, I'll never be as good as you.

Sister Mary Brass Knuckles

Back when dinosaurs roamed the earth and I was attending elementary school, there were only two teachers for every grade. This left students with two simple options each year: we either got the good teacher or the bad teacher.

At my school, the good teacher was usually a fresh-faced young woman just out of college. More often than not, the bad teacher was a nun. Good teachers smelled like flowers and passed out chocolate suckers to everyone on Valentine's Day. The nuns smelled like window cleaner and were prone to spontaneous displays of fury.

For reasons that still remain a mystery to me, I always got the bad teacher. This led me to recite some very unusual nightly prayers. "Please, God," I'd pray. "Please let Sister Mary Brass Knuckles fall down the steps of the convent. I don't want her to die or anything; I just want her to be in enough pain to miss the rest of the school year. Oh, and please let the Sabres win the Stanley Cup. Amen."

Just as God never answered those prayers, my mom never answered my desperate pleas to call my school and convince the principal to place me in Miss Smellsnice's classroom. My mom believed that when it came to evaluating what was best for me in school, no one knew me better than my teachers. For seven hours a day, five days a week and 36 weeks a year, my teachers observed me in the classroom. When it came to deciding whose classroom I would be placed in the following year, they knew whether I needed a Miss Smellsnice or a Sister Mary Brass Knuckles.

Back then, the relationship between school and home was generally filled with mutual respect and cooperation. The principal at my school had no interest in telling my mom how to run her family and my mom had no interest in telling my principal how to run her school.

Things are different now. A friend of mine who is a teacher estimates that at least 30 percent of the parents in her school make teacher requests for their child. If my friend's calculations are correct, roughly 150 parents in her school are deluded enough to believe that they know enough about how their child functions in a school environment to decide who their teacher should be in the following school year.

It should come as no surprise to anyone that over the past decade, my friend has never had a parent request that their child be placed in the classroom of a teacher who is perceived to be strict or demanding. The parents who make teacher requests are always looking for a Miss Smellsnice. According to my friend, requests rarely serve the best interests of a child. Teacher requests are thinly veiled popularity contests.

In the interest of full disclosure, my wife and I once came pretty close to requesting that our child be placed in a popular teacher's classroom. When our daughter was entering first grade, we desperately wanted her to be placed in the classroom of a teacher I'll call Mrs. T.

Mrs. T was the most popular in the school for a reason. She was a teacher's teacher, a cross between Julie Andrews and Eleanor Roosevelt. Children flocked to her and many adults did, too. Whenever I was lucky enough to stop and talk with her in the hallway, I had an overwhelming urge to have Mrs. T bake me chocolate chip cookies and read me a story.

As our daughter approached the midpoint of kindergarten, we learned that loads of parents were lobbying the principal to find a spot for their child in Mrs. T's classroom. Should we swallow our principles and make our plea to the principal?

We didn't make the call and Molly was placed in the classroom of the Other Teacher, a woman I'll call Mrs. G. Among other personality quirks, Mrs. G smelled like cigarettes, snapped her gum, and rarely remembered the first names of her students. Every child in her classroom was either "him," "her," or "that one."

Shortly after school started, Tricia and I were telling our tale of woe to a friend of ours and she forcefully set us straight. I'll concede that Mrs. G is a little nutty, our friend said, but that woman could teach a brick wall how to read. She maintained that Mrs. G was the best reading teacher in the entire school— even better than the legendary Mrs. T.

She was right. Despite a wide array of borderline personality disorders, Mrs. G was also, in her own way, a teacher's teacher. She had a unique ability to connect with children of all backgrounds and talents. By the end of the year, every single student in her classroom was reading above grade level.

At the time, my wife and I had a combined 30 years of experience working with tens of thousands of children in a variety of physical education settings, yet we had no clue as to which first grade teacher would be best for our little girl.

Though I'm thankful that my wife and I kept our noses out of the principal's office, sometimes I wonder if we're ignoring a golden opportunity here. There is an obvious new revenue stream available to any school district facing a budget crisis and the name of the revenue stream is Teacher Auctions.

Why not parade an entire faculty in front of an auditorium full of parents at the beginning of the school year and auction off spots in the classrooms of the most popular teachers in school? My guess is that there would be hundreds of misguided helicopter parents willing to pay any price to get their child a year with Miss Smellsnice. The school district would keep the extra revenue, taxes would be kept in check, and thousands of myopic, hyper-competitive parents would rest easy with the belief that their child was being taught by the best teacher money can buy.

What happens to those children whose parents aren't willing to refinance their mortgages for a desk in Miss Smellsnice's classroom? It's my experience that most of those students will receive fewer gold stars, fewer pats on the head—and an excellent education. For the most effective teachers I have met in my travels had no interest in what their students or their students' parents thought of them. Great teachers don't use a classroom as a vehicle to win popularity contests; they use their classroom as a vehicle to teach.

The Bad Kid

For roughly 12 weeks back in the summer of 1972, my best friend was the baddest kid on the planet. Even at the tender age of eight, Tommy Wolff seemed intent on committing at least one misdemeanor a day. If he wasn't stealing candy from our neighborhood convenience store, he was shooting squirrels with his BB gun. No one was exempt from his daily crime spree. Not parents, not teachers, and certainly not small animals.

Why did I want to be friends with a kid who liked to steal and spill squirrel blood? The most obvious reason was that Tommy's family had one of those gigantic rectangular pools with an automatic vacuum and a redwood deck. Being a silent accomplice to Tommy's life of crime seemed like a reasonable price to pay for the privilege of floating around in the Wolff family pool every day.

The other reason why I wanted to be Tommy's friend was that it was fun to hang out with a bad kid. Years of faithful attendance at a Catholic elementary school had taught me that I'd risk eternal damnation if I stole a comic book or told a lie. Concepts like eternal damnation and breaking commandments seemed lost on Tommy. He lived life without a conscience and in turn, without fear and guilt. Part of me believed that my friend was going straight to hell and part of me wanted to be just like him.

Our friendship ended when Tommy's crime sprees started to extend to my baseball card collection and eventually, the big ceramic mug where I kept my allowance money. He denied it, but I knew he was stealing from me. Once I was Tommy's victim, hanging out in the bad kid's pool lost its appeal. Things ended for good when he stole my Brooks Robinson rookie card. Whether you're eight or 88, a guy has to draw the line somewhere.

As much as I'd still like to have those baseball cards back, I don't regret being Tommy Wolff's friend. Looking back, I realize that meeting a guy who wasn't a good friend was just as important as meeting a guy who was. In a weird way, I'm thankful that he stole my allowance money. I'm even more thankful that my mom allowed me the freedom to make my own friends—and my own mistakes.

Sadly, this is a freedom that my wife and I never extended to our own son. Throughout his childhood, we subtly steered Zac toward friends that had the Tim and Tricia Hirschbeck Seal of Approval. If he wanted to go to the movies with a friend who regularly said "please" and "thank you," we were happy to give them a ride and a few bucks for the snack bar. If he wanted to hang out with a kid who wore a Stone Cold Steve Austin t-shirt and spit a lot, we always seemed to have a scheduling conflict.

Ten years ago, it seemed like a good idea to try to connect Zac with good kids. Today, I'm wondering if all that well-intentioned matchmaking will inhibit his ability to deal with the Tommy Wolffs of this world later on in life. Sooner or later, we're all forced to develop the skills to deal with the baddest kid on the planet. Isn't it easier to develop those skills in kindergarten than in college?

Look, I'm not suggesting that we should encourage our kids to befriend the neighborhood juvenile delinquent. The suggestion from here is that we recognize that there is a serious downside to micromanaging a child's relationships. If your son happens to know a kid who has a BB gun and a Brooks Robinson rookie card, it might be the best friend he'll ever make.

Someday You'll Thank Me For This

I'm walking out of Kenmore Middle School last May after dropping our little 13-year-old ball of teenage angst off for a class camping trip when I come upon a sign posted next to the Guidance Office. Printed on the sign was a list of the Top 10 students in each grade. I skim through the list looking to see if I recognize any friends or former players when, lo and behold, what name should magically appear as the eighth-ranked student of a few hundred kids in her seventh-grade class?

Molly Hirschbeck.

It was what my wife and I call a parenting moment, a brief period of clarity amidst the chaos of raising children when you realize that all of your hard work is paying off. Molly is only 13 and I guess there's still plenty of time for her to turn into a drug dealer, or worse yet, a U.S. senator. Yet it's easy to look at our beautiful daughter these days and think two thoughts: we are truly blessed and we must be doing something right.

Molly wasn't always a good student. There was a time not too long ago when she was much more interested in chatting with her friends and obsessing over the latest classroom romance than completing her homework. A few nights ago, Tricia and I were trying to figure out when Molly changed over from a social butterfly to an excellent student. For me, that moment came on a bright, sunny morning in September 1995.

Fourth grade was the first year Molly started to bring home a substantial amount of homework each night and at first, she struggled mightily to accept her new responsibilities. Almost every morning at the beginning of the school year, we'd follow the same script:

Molly would remember that she had forgotten to complete an assignment.

Tricia and I would get upset and tell her that this wasn't acceptable.

Our 4-year-old son, Zac, would ask if he could have another bagel.

After a week of this continuing melodrama, Tricia and I decided that enough was enough. We sat Molly down at the dining room table and told her that she was to complete all of her homework immediately after getting home from school. Upon completing her homework, she needed to double-check her work and make sure all of her assignments were completed before she did anything else that afternoon. If she woke up in the morning and found she had forgotten to complete an assignment, she would stay at home and complete her homework before going to school that day.

You can imagine what happened next. A week later, I'm walking up our basement stairs around 8:30 a.m. when our tearful daughter appears at the top of the stairs and screams, "DADIFORGOTTODOMYMATHPROBLEMS!!!!!!!!!"

"OK," I said. "I'll call the school and tell them you'll be late. You'd better get to work." For the next 45 minutes, Molly went into hysterics. She cried, she wailed, and she begged for one last chance. When begging and tears didn't work, the accusations started to fly. I wasn't being fair, we were bad parents, and none of her other friend's parents would ever do something like this to their daughter. My wife and I refused to argue or negotiate with Molly. We waited. And waited. And waited some more. After all was said and done, it took Molly two hours to complete 15 simple math problems.

When Tricia finally dropped Molly off at school, her teacher immediately stepped out into the hall to welcome our still-tearful daughter to school. Desperately searching for an ally in her battle against her cruel parents, Molly tearfully told Mrs. Roaldi about the brutality that her parents had put her through that morning. Mrs. Roaldi could have said something like, "It sounds like you've had a tough morning, honey" or "I'm sorry you've had a bad day, but I'm glad you're here now." Either statement would have been perfectly acceptable. Instead, she bent down, looked Molly right in the eye and said, "Well, Molly, it sounds to me like your parents love you very much." It was the perfect response.

Once Molly understood that her parents and teacher were a united front, she ran out of places to point fingers. Together, we forced our kid to accept responsibility for her own actions. At that moment, a dozen essential messages about life and school connected in Molly's head. Chief among them:

- *It is Molly's responsibility to complete her assigned homework on time.*
- *There will be serious ramifications if she does not accept her responsibilities in school.*
- *When her mom and dad say something, they mean it.*
- *Her teacher and parents are not adversaries and they will not be turned against each other.*
- *Even though it might seem like her parents or teachers are mean or unfair at times, their decisions are always made with Molly's best interests at heart.*

Molly has never forgotten to complete a homework assignment since that day. She has always earned excellent grades and received great reports from her teachers. Most of the credit for that good news traces its way back to Molly. In the end, she makes the daily decision as to whether she is a productive or a lazy student. Still, my guess is that our daughter's name wouldn't have been up on that bulletin board if we had made a different decision on that sunny September morning.

It would have been so easy to wimp out, to have dried Molly's tears, given her a stern warning and sent her off to school on time. And it would have been so easy for Mrs. Roaldi to put a comforting arm around Molly's shoulders without supporting us. Smiles would have replaced tears and kind words would have replaced sobs and accusations. Everyone would have felt good about themselves—for a few weeks. All of those important lessons would have gotten lost and been replaced by the following harmful messages:

- *It is her parent's responsibility to nag, threaten and remind her to complete her assigned homework on time.*
- *There might be some repercussions if she does not accept her responsibilities in school. Then again, maybe not.*
- *When her mom and dad say something, they might mean it. Then again, they might not.*
- *Her parents are so afraid of being viewed as mean or unfair that they will do almost anything to keep a smile on her face.*

"Someday you'll thank me for this."

If you were born prior to 1970, chances are that your mom and dad said that to you a few thousand times when you were a kid. It was their mantra, a secret psalm with no real rhyme or reason and each time they said it, they probably drove you half crazy.

But they were right. Our moms and dads understood that there wasn't a lot of instant gratification when it came to raising a child. They understood that the rewards of parenting came 10 or 20 years down the road when your child became a responsible student, dedicated professional or a faithful spouse. Over the course of that journey, it was expected that there would be plenty of times when your child would not only think you were unfair and unreasonable, they would hate your guts.

My generation of parents doesn't understand the concept of "Someday you'll thank me for this." The thought that our child might hate our guts ties our stomach up in knots. It haunts us. We want a smile on our child's face, we want the smile right now, and we want that smile to stay there. We'll let a 13-year-old hang out at the mall all weekend, walk around with their pants halfway down their ass, and pick them up in limos on their birthday before we'll say "no" to them.

Tricia and I have made tons of mistakes with our two kids, but one mistake that we've never made is wanting Molly and Zac to like us. We have no desire to be their friend or confidante. From the moment they first opened their eyes into a big new world, all we ever wanted to be was their mom and dad. Sometimes that means making decisions that are unpopular and sometimes that means having our son and daughter hate our guts, but that's the price you pay to raise a loving and responsible child.

They might hate us today, but someday they'll thank us for this.

The Enemy

The list of grievances is extensive:

He is a screamer.

He tells anyone who will listen that having fun is more important than winning, yet he places enormous pressure on his players to win.

He preaches the virtues of fitness and endurance, yet weighs a few dozen donuts over 300 pounds.

He treats his strongest players like kings and his weakest players like cattle.

He is a name-dropper.

He treats the dads on his team like drinking buddies and the moms like morons.

At games and practices, he always wears a full uniform on the sidelines.

It was shortly after I walked by one of his practices and heard him tell an overweight nine-year-old boy he was "nothing more than a big waste of space" that I decided that I needed to beat him. Listening to him belittle a third-grader made things personal. Suddenly, he morphed into the sum total of every obnoxious teacher, coach, and parent that had ever treated me harshly when I was a kid. He was no longer just another coach in the league, he was The Enemy.

My goal for our game transitioned from simple defeat to decisive victory to complete and unconditional domination. As the contest drew closer, my coaching style transitioned from Joe Torre to Mike Ditka to Joseph Stalin.

Six weeks before we were scheduled to play The Enemy's team, he started to occupy my thoughts every single day. Sometimes it was only a passing thought about what I'd say to him as we shook hands after the game, but on more occasions than I'd care to admit, I'd spend considerable amounts of time trying to get inside his head. The FBI would have been envious of the back-story I created to explain how The Enemy turned out the way he did. His desire to wear a full uniform on the sidelines was more than a little strange; I'd have bet money that he had never put on a jersey and played organized sports when he was a kid. His open contempt for women led me to believe that he had an uneasy relationship with his mother and probably didn't kiss a girl until junior year of college. The combination of his weight and quick temper led me to believe that he was carrying around some serious emotional baggage. My sense was that he was the fat guy that got picked on a lot in high school, the sort of guy who got food thrown at him in the lunchroom at least once or twice a month.

After poring over all the data I had assembled in The Enemy's case file, I figured that the key to beating him was to make him play from behind. He didn't strike me as a guy who had much experience playing games that mattered. If we could score a couple of early goals, I figured that The Enemy would lose his composure and his team would fall apart.

And that's exactly what happened. We scored two goals in the first 10 minutes of what had, in my mind at least, turned from a 10-under soccer game into The Epic Struggle Between Good and Evil. As predicted, The Enemy did not handle adversity well. He screamed, he argued, he threw a couple of tantrums, and after our team went up 5-1 in the second half, he just sort of gave up. When I shook his hand afterwards, I had a smug and satisfied smile on my face.

My purpose in sharing this story with you is not to boast about my abilities as a tactician or tell you a heartwarming tale about the time I beat the big, bad coach. Instead, it is offered as evidence that with very little provocation, I am capable of being a complete idiot. The Epic Struggle Between Good and Evil took place several years ago, but it still haunts me. When I think of The Enemy and my childish obsession with beating him, I'm reminded that the only real enemy I have ever encountered in youth sports is myself.

I've met ethical and hardworking coaches who inspire me and sleazy coaches who would sell their wife to win a T-ball game played by five- and six-year-olds. I've met parents who set a shining example for their sons and daughters every day of the week and ignorant moms and dads who proudly hurl profanities at a referee in front of a group of 10-year-olds. I've worked for league administrators who constantly search for new ways to improve their club and administrators who constantly search for new ways to get their photo in the newspaper. The only constant in the parade of the saints and scumbags I've met in youth sports over the years is me. I'm the guy who controls how much I support and appreciate the great people I meet, and I'm the guy who controls how I react to The Enemy—in all its incarnations.

When I heard that coach tell a nine-year-old kid he was basically worthless, I could have taken at least a dozen constructive actions. Speaking to the coach and telling him how his words sounded to a passerby's ears might have been helpful. Talking to the league's director or working to create a basic training program for the league's coaches might have ultimately helped hundreds of coaches. Perhaps the most important thing I could have done was establish contact with the nine-year-old kid to make sure he understood that he wasn't a waste of space.

Instead, I chose to construct a quiet, personal vendetta against a fellow coach. My team won a game by four goals, but I was the biggest loser on the field.

Accoutrements

Youth sports used to be so simple. Practice, play, and go home.

Things are a little more complicated today. For example, what sport are you interested in playing? Are you interested in baseball, football, soccer, basketball, softball, T-ball, hockey, swimming, volleyball, golf, tennis, lacrosse, gymnastics, rugby, and/or cheerleading?

Once you choose a sport to play, it's time to figure out how good you are. Welcome to the world of try-outs, cuts, practices, games, practice games, scrimmages, A leagues, B leagues, recreational leagues, developmental leagues, house leagues, instructional leagues, travel teams, all-star teams, premier teams, camps, specialty camps, goalkeeping academies, and hitting clinics.

Now that we've established your skill level, it's time to figure out where you'll be playing. Does your team play indoors or outdoors? On natural grass or artificial turf? During the day or under the lights at night? Locally, regionally, or nationally? Do you play in a gym, on a field, in a rink, at a training center, in a dome, at a multi-purpose sports facility, in an arena, or at a stadium? Does the facility have locker rooms, showers, bathrooms, stretching rooms, warm-up rooms, or all of the above? If you or your parents are hungry, does the facility have a restaurant, snack bar, vending machines, or are you forced to bring food from home? Here is the multi-million dollar question: is the facility privately owned or publicly funded by taxes?

Whoever said "It doesn't matter whether you win or lose, it's how you play the game" must have been playing a long time ago, because today's leagues are likely to contain winners, losers, league standings, rankings, scorebooks, overtime, double overtime, sudden-death overtime, shoot-outs, extra innings, single elimination, double elimination, challenge ladders, rankings, playoffs, championships, consolation rounds, tournaments, round-robin tournaments, regional tournaments, and showcase tournaments.

Your league is only legitimate if there are at least 342 adults running things. How many coaches, managers, assistant coaches, assistant mangers, trainers, clinicians, referees, umpires, officials, judges, marshals, administrators, coordinators, organizers, fundraisers, board members, board liaisons, committee members, sub-committee members, and ad hoc sub-committee troubleshooters are responsible for making sure that things run according to plan?

How many organizational meetings, board meetings, planning meetings, officials meetings, scheduling meetings, team meetings, parent meetings, league meetings, fundraising meetings, committee meetings, equipment meetings, seminars, clinics, camps, conferences, conventions, and trainings are scheduled to make sure your league runs smoothly?

How much money do your parents pay for the privilege of watching you play sports? Do they just pay a registration fee or do they have to write checks for league fees, team fees, tournament fees, administration fees, equipment fees, insurance fees, uniform fees, maintenance fees, travel fees, and capital development fees?

Sports isn't about giving, it's about getting. Does your team give you home uniforms, away uniforms, training uniforms, warm-up suits, team jackets, equipment bags, and equipment to put in your equipment bags? At the end of the season, do you get trophies, plaques, ribbons, medals, certificates, patches, pins, cups, bowls, flags, water bottles, engraved bats, autograph books, or team photos?

How do your parents pay for all of the stuff you get? Does your team sell raffle tickets, candy bars, baked goods, donuts, wrapping paper, coupon books or popcorn? Do your parents run car washes, fish fry dinners, pancake breakfasts, chicken barbecues, spaghetti dinners, auctions, ice cream socials, craft fairs, or dances to raise money for your team?

Now that your season is starting, don't forget to prepare for the game. Get at least eight hours of sleep, eat a nutritious breakfast, take your vitamins, lather yourself with sunscreen, and bring water or a sports drink with you to the game. If it's your turn to bring a snack for everyone after the game, please tell your parents that orange slices, frozen juice bars, granola bars, pretzels, yogurt, juice, and sports drinks are recommended post game snacks. Candy, pop, gum, popsicles, and chips are frowned upon. There is a pizza party at the Ferguson's next Thursday, and the coach is taking everyone out for ice cream on the 21st.

Let's take a look at you. Aren't you going to wear something underneath your jersey? Where is your equipment bag? Do you have your cleats? Are you really going to go to the game with your hair looking like that? Please tuck in your uniform and remember to double-knot your cleats. Can you get my chair out of the closet? Do you think we need an umbrella? Is the team you're playing tonight a good team?

Looks like we're finally ready. Have a good game tonight—and remember, the most important part of playing the game is to just have fun.

The Boy Behind The Mask

For over a decade, I coordinated summer camp programs for a local non-profit organization here in the area. It would be up to other people to judge whether or not I was a good camp director, but I certainly loved my work. Once the intoxicating elixir of bug juice and chlorine seeps into your veins, it changes you forever.

For me, a good summer camp was a mix of all the best things in life: love, friendship, courage, art, music, teamwork, laughter, mystery, tears, and so much more. I love my current job and it has been 19 years since I last worked camp. Yet even today, when school lets out every June, my thoughts still wander to campfires, friendship bracelets, and Craig Scibetta Day.

Most of you know what a friendship bracelet is and for your own sake, I hope you know how to make a campfire. You're probably a little less familiar with the splendor and spectacle of Craig Scibetta Day.

Young Mr. Scibetta was one of my favorite all-time campers. He embodied all the good that summer camp can do for a kid. When I first met him, he was a shy, skinny, seven-year-old camper with a bad haircut and a lousy attitude. He was prone to mumbling "I hate this" or "this stinks" every 10 minutes and he always wore one of those big black Texas Instrument digital watches—even in the pool. Craig's wrists were so small that his watch looked a radial tire wrapped around a #2 pencil.

It didn't happen overnight, but Craig eventually warmed up to camp. Someone on our staff found out that he was interested in acting and with very little prodding from us, he became a regular star of the camp skits and talent shows that we'd run every week. Most of the guys wanted to hang out with him because he was funny in a milk-coming-out-of-your-nose kind of way. The girls liked him because he was cute and entertaining without being particularly threatening.

Years passed and it wasn't long before Craig the Camper morphed into Craig the Counselor. The Texas Instrument watch, bad haircut and lousy attitude quickly became a thing of the past. As a counselor, Craig was a "kid magnet". It didn't matter if he was in the pool, the arts and crafts tent, or the lunch table; wherever he went, Craig always had at least four campers grafted to his hip. The campers loved him for lots of reasons. He was creative, funny, and unlike most counselors his age, willing to make a complete fool of himself in front of large groups of people. If campers were extremely shy or nervous, Craig would do just about anything to make them laugh.

I'm not sure who came up with the idea for Craig Scibetta Day. I remember that it was near the end of the summer and our brains were fried. It had been an unusually wet summer and everyone on our staff had racked their brains coming up with special themes and activities to keep the campers entertained and dodging the raindrops. We'd done Backwards Day, Christmas In July, Board Game Olympics, Water Week and just about every other traditional camp theme we could think of.

At a staff meeting, someone jokingly suggested that we devote an entire camp day to honor Craig Scibetta. We all laughed at first, but the more we thought about it, the more we realized that the idea could work. Besides, did I mention that we were really desperate?

The first time that we held Craig Scibetta Day, the rules were pretty simple. We explained to the campers that Craig had met a magical genie and had been granted one wish: to be the all-powerful ruler of our camp for one day. If Craig told a camper to do something, they were obligated to honor his request or risk being cursed forever.

For the next 24 hours, Craig pretended to be a kinder, gentler version of Rasputin. No one escaped his reign of terror. He directed that all the 11- and 12-year-old boys play a Duck, Duck, Goose tournament in his honor. He demanded that the assistant camp director feed him grapes at lunch. The five- and six-year-old girls were commissioned to make the new Craig Scibetta camp flag. I was directed to do 20 push ups at lunch because I failed to address Craig as "Your Royal Highness."

The campers went absolutely nuts. Part of them lived in fear that Craig would ask them to do something crazy, and part of them lived in fear that he wouldn't. Throughout the day, everyone was on the edge of their seats to see what His Royal Highness would do next.

The ceremonies surrounding Craig Scibetta Day quickly became the stuff of legend. For the veteran campers and staff that returned to our camp every year, Craig Scibetta Day was the day that they looked forward to more than any other. One of my most treasured camp souvenirs is a photo taken of the 1990 Craig Scibetta Day. All 120 campers and 30 staff are proudly wearing their Craig Scibetta masks made out of paper plates. Our masks cover our faces, but you can tell that all of us are smiling.

One week after that photo was taken, my camp director days were over.

I quit working camp for a variety of reasons. Once my daughter was born, it was tough to be away from home so much. I still loved working at camp, but I missed my girls.

I also sensed that there were some pretty ugly trends taking shape in summer camps all across America. Up until the mid-1980s, folks always recognized that one of the best things about summer camp was that it wasn't school. For 10 months out of the year, we forced our kids to sit at a wooden desk housed inside a big box housed inside an even bigger box. Once a child stepped inside that box every morning, there was little room for creativity and spontaneity.

Camp was all about creativity, spontaneity, and fun. The way I saw it, my job as a camp director was to give the campers a general structure for camp, make sure that they were safe, and then get the hell out of their way. Freedom, nonsense, and even a little anarchy used to be essential elements of summer camp.

In today's environment, freedom and spontaneity are still wonderful things—as long as they occur in a hermetically sealed cabin with a surveillance camera and four camp staff peering over a camper's shoulder.

For me, the end came in an air-conditioned office, sitting across the table from a woman who had been out to visit our camp exactly once in three years. She loved me because there were always 30 to 40 kids on a waiting list to get into our camp, but she was concerned that our camp wasn't "educational" enough for the kids.

I remember sitting at her desk as she held up a Craig Scibetta mask like it was a dirty diaper. "Tim," she said, "what is the purpose of this?"

"That was for the 5th Annual Craig Scibetta Day!" I laughed. "The kids love it." I explained the origins and traditions associated with the activity and invited her to come out and meet Craig at our end-of-the-summer party.

"But what are the goals and objectives of this activity?" she asked. Maybe my head was feeling the effects of a summer full of bug juice consumption, but I was struggling to understand her question.

"What do you mean?" I asked.

"What is the purpose of this activity?" she asked. I could tell she was starting to get frustrated with me because she was speaking to me like I was a five-year-old. "What is the purpose of making masks that look like this Craig boy?"

"To have fun."

She looked at me like I was speaking a foreign language.

Looking back, I guess I was.

Pay Me My Money Down

For the first four or five years of owning our own business, Tricia and I really struggled to make ends meet. We both had spent over a decade working at a local non-profit organization. While working in the non-profit sector was fun and rewarding, it was not exactly a source of overwhelming financial reward. When we left our jobs and decided to venture into the world of the self-employed, both of us were forced to exhaust our retirement savings and accumulate some pretty serious debt in order to keep our company afloat.

Back then, our primary source of transportation was a light blue 1984 Nissan Sentra with over 75,000 miles on it. There are two things that you should know about that Sentra. The first is that from the moment that Tricia and I proudly drove it off the dealer's lot, it rapidly started to rust from the inside out. The second is that the car was possessed by demons that were bent on breaking my will.

I hated that car. I hated how it would taunt me by gasping and gurgling every time I accelerated over 50 miles per hour. I hated how it would stall out at stoplights every time it rained or snowed. Mostly, I hated how it would hack and cough for a few seconds every time I turned the engine off, as if to say "I'm feeling (gasp) a little under the weather, Tim. Not sure if (cough, cough) I'll be able to (gasp) start up tomorrow."

By 1995, our company had expanded into snow country and we were faced with an interesting dilemma. Was it nobler to stare death in the face every time we took the Sentra on the I-90 or spend money we didn't have to lease a new car that would safely get us where we needed to go? Both of us hated the idea of going into more debt, but both of us knew that it was better to take a financial risk and possibly live to see our grandchildren than to drive the Sentra over snow-covered roads on a regular basis.

So we leased a car—a gold Mazda MPV. Tricia liked the idea of having a minivan to transport equipment and the kids. I liked the idea of having four-wheel-drive in the winter. Both of us worried about the money, but both of us also loved breathing in that new car smell.

Shortly after we signed the papers on the car, the dad of one of my players walked by me after practice and made one of those snarky jokes that isn't really a joke, "Nice car, Tim!" he called out. "Now I can see where all my registration fees are going!" The not-so-subtle message behind the not-really-a-joke was that guys who teach kids to play sports for a living shouldn't be making enough money to lease a new minivan.

If I had been the guy who sold Mr. Snark his insurance policy or the guy who installed new gutters on his house, he wouldn't have felt compelled to comment on my new car. If I had been the guy who cooked him a really nice meal at his favorite restaurant, he might have even congratulated me on the MPV. But because I taught his son how to play sports, he was clearly uncomfortable with my supposed success. In Mr. Snark's world, it was socially acceptable for men and women to make a good living selling insurance, gutters, or minestrone soup. Guys who taught kids how to play sports should work for free.

One of the few universal youth sports lessons I have learned over the past three decades is this: the most important element of a strong youth sports league is coaching. More than cool uniforms or million-dollar playing facilities, the success of a league is directly related to the quality of instruction and leadership that players receive from their coach. It is the coach who decides the material that will be covered in each practice, assigns playing time and positions to each player on the team, dictates the goals and philosophy of the team, and holds players and parents accountable for their actions and behavior.

With so much responsibility resting on the shoulders of youth coaches, why do we insist that coaching children must be an act of noble volunteerism? Where is it written that teaching a child how to dissect a frog should earn a teacher a competitive salary-and-benefits package, but teaching a child how to function as a member of a team should earn a coach a thank-you card and a gift certificate to a local restaurant?

Over the years, I've spent a considerable amount of time on both sides of the volunteer fence. Years ago, my job description included the recruitment, training, and supervision of hundreds of volunteers. Many of the volunteer coaches I worked with years ago are still good friends and I'm forever grateful that they were kind enough to donate their time and talent to the players in our league.

Yet it would be foolish to pretend that there aren't serious challenges facing any organization that relies exclusively on volunteers. One of the biggest problems I always faced was turnover. Volunteer coaches usually coached their own kids which meant that their commitment to coach in the league was directly related to their child. If the child was totally invested in playing, I might be able to count on the mom or dad to coach in the league for four to six years. If the child wasn't particularly invested, the coach was gone after three months. It always seemed like I was scrambling to replace coaches every season.

Inevitably, dealing with a high turnover rate led me to reduce the expectations I had for my coaches. Because I was constantly begging parents to volunteer, I embraced barely competent coaches and tolerated incompetent ones. Everyone in our organization resisted holding our coaches to higher standards because we lived in fear that one or two or 12 of them might quit.

Instead of expecting our coaches to attend training sessions and obtain basic first aid certifications, I coddled them. Many of the coaches that I worked with had a list of requests that required my attention. John wanted two boys who were late to sign up to play on his team; Ellen wanted to practice on the best fields at the best time slots; Bill wanted jackets for his coaches; Tony insisted that his son play the whole game every game. Youth sports coaches and administrators are different from many types of volunteers in that they usually expect some type of special attention. If parents volunteer at a local hospital, they don't expect better medical treatment for their families in return. But in youth sports, the common expectation is that those who volunteer to coach deserve some sort of preferential treatment.

If it sounds like I'm attacking volunteer coaches, that's not my intent. Every community contains dedicated and talented volunteers who deserve to be placed on top of the tallest fire truck in town and given a parade in their honor. Filling a league with volunteer coaches isn't necessarily a bad option, but it should never be the only option.

Most leagues spend most of their money on their facilities, uniforms, and trophies while insisting that coaches volunteer their services. When I began to run leagues of my own, I was interested in spending most of our money on coaches and very little on all the other stuff that didn't seem to matter all that much to the kids.

Almost overnight, giving coaches financial compensation solved 90 percent of the problems I had always experienced in running youth sports leagues. The days of begging moms and dads to help out and coach a team were over. Instead of gratefully accepting any warm body that was kind enough to volunteer, I was able to screen applicants and conduct interviews with the best candidates. For every open coaching spot in our league, I had at least a dozen job applications sitting on my desk.

The candidates who made it through the selection process were usually excellent coaches who were interested in becoming even better. Everyone was receptive to constructive criticism and parent evaluations. Nobody balked at attending training and certification sessions. For the first time, I was allowed to have high expectations of our coaches and for the first time, I was surrounded by men and women who were interested in meeting those expectations.

The most surprising benefit of paying our coaches was that no one expected any type of preferential treatment. The only special privilege my coaches expected from me was the ability to continue earning $15 an hour at a job that was fun and rewarding.

None of the new coaches I hired coached their own children, which created a more cooperative and healthy atmosphere among our coaching staff. No one secretly wanted his or her kid to be the star of the team, no one was heavily invested in drafting a team of all-stars, and no one harbored a grudge against another coach or team. There weren't any petty rivalries or political maneuverings that sometimes infest youth sports. Our staff of coaches was truly a team committed to serving the best interests of all the players in our league.

Over the past 20 years, every league I've run has been led by a small partnership of talented coaches earning a competitive wage. Money hasn't made all of the traditional problems commonly associated with youth sports go away, but it has helped to insure that they rear their ugly heads less often. If given the choice between working with a group of committed volunteer coaches or a staff of dedicated coaches earning $15 an hour, show me the money.

1972

Between 1969 and 1979, most of my days were spent playing ball on the streets and fields that surround Longfellow Elementary, formerly a small elementary school less than a block away from my house.

The games that my friends and I played varied from season to season. Baseball dominated our after school schedule from June to August; touch and tackle football in the fall; street hockey games in the Longfellow parking lot during the winter; and basketball in my friend Eddie's backyard during the spring. On those days when we needed a change of pace, we'd head over to the playground next to Longfellow and play games like Capture the Flag, Kick the Can and Hide and Seek.

The neighborhood pick-up games of my youth were about much more than just playing sports. We learned how to recruit players, organize the game, deal with arguments, and manage the game so that everyone wanted to play. Perhaps the greatest skill we learned was the ability to communicate and cooperate with other kids without direction from our parents. Sometimes it was a very delicate balancing act to keep the game going, and sometimes everyone quit and went home. Playing sports was filled with success and failure, and it all belonged to us.

Though my son has been raised in a home located only 300 yards from the house I grew up in, Zac has never played Kick the Can or gathered a dozen friends to play baseball over at Longfellow. He's not allowed to play hockey in the street or make his own friends. My wife and I pay large sums of money for the privilege of passively controlling which sports he plays, who he plays with, where he plays, and when his games are scheduled.

Last night, my wife and I went for a walk around the neighborhood and found ourselves standing by the playground at Longfellow. It was a warm summer night, the sun was still two hours away from plunging into the horizon, and Longfellow was completely deserted. How did youth sports change so radically in the span of a single generation? When did street football turn into a death sentence? Why did adults assume so much control over the games our children play?

I blame everything on Roone Arledge.

Do you remember him? He was the brilliant television executive who created "ABC's Wide World Of Sports," "Monday Night Football," "Nightline," and "ABC World News Tonight." Widely credited with inventing instant replay and slow motion, Arledge didn't just change the way we looked at sports, he changed the way that we looked at the world.

One of the signature touches that Arledge brought to ABC's Olympics coverage was a feature called "Up Close and Personal." The idea of these two- to three-minute segments was to give the viewer at home a behind-the-scenes look at an athlete's life away from the playing field. Sometimes an Up Close and Personal segment would deal with an overwhelming obstacle that a player overcame on their way to becoming a world-class athlete, but more often than not, the segments focused on a player's training and preparation for their big moment.

Throughout the 1972 Olympics, ABC pushed the Up Close and Personal button repeatedly. American viewers watched Mark Spitz, the winner of seven gold medals for swimming in the '72 Games, tell an emotional story of his father moving the entire Spitz family to Santa Clara, California, so that Mark could be close to the best swimming training in the nation. Network cameras became infatuated with the rigorous training regimens of tiny gymnasts from communist nations, particularly a 17-year-old Soviet gymnast named Olga Korbut. Prior to Korbut's first Olympic appearance in '72, there were 15,000 practicing gymnasts in the United States. A decade later, the number had grown to over 200,000.

Suddenly, a new narrative was created for building strong athletes. Place children in a heavily competitive environment at an early age, surround them with as much structure and training as they can bear, and watch the cream rise to the top.

The Up Close and Personal stories of Spitz and Korbut made being a world-class athlete seem like an accessible goal for every parent and child willing to turn their lives over to youth sports. Suddenly, men and women were adjusting their lives to immerse themselves in the games that their children were playing. A new breed of youth sports parent began to appear on the American landscape. The dad who came home from work, had a drink and read the newspaper on the front porch was replaced by the dad who quit his job, sold his house, and moved to another state so his son could receive the best training money could buy. The mom who generally ignored her child's participation in youth sports leagues was replaced by the mom who was totally invested in coordinating her child's participation in youth sports leagues.

Before the 1970's came to an end, the oppressive presence of adults in youth sports could be felt everywhere. The simple act of playing a game of baseball or football now required registration, administration, transportation, legislation, promotion, and scheduling. The game was now controlled by directors and coordinators, coaches and assistant coaches, referees and officials. For the first time in history, playing sports was no longer an activity that belonged exclusively to kids.

One of the first things that adults brought to youth sports was more rules. When children were left alone to control their own games, the rules were usually flexible. An uneven number of players would lead to an all-time pitcher or quarterback. New teams could be chosen in the middle of a game if one team was killing the other. Shouting out "next touchdown wins" or "gotta win by two" could bring new excitement and urgency to a game. It was understood that if the game wasn't fun and fair, no one would want to play.

As adults began to immerse themselves in youth sports, the rules of the game became rigid. Every team was required to carry a roster of players that met specific residency requirements and age restrictions. Even when teams were seriously unbalanced, rosters were kept intact through an entire season. It was understood that if the game wasn't fun and fair, it would be played anyway.

Sometimes the score of our neighborhood games mattered a lot and sometimes it didn't. When adults took over youth sports, the score became the primary focus of playing sports. Standings were always tracked and posted. Playoffs and championships—even at very young age levels—became much more widespread. Eventually, being the best team in your community became an incidental accomplishment instead of an honor. Travel leagues and all-star teams were constructed to determine who was the best team in the region, state, and country.

Along with competition to be the best team or club in a region came competition to play games in the best facilities. Grass fields and school gymnasiums became outdated venues for youth sports contests. Million-dollar playing facilities outfitted with state-of-the-art playing surfaces, lighting, locker rooms, and restaurants began to spring up everywhere. Where a child played became almost as important as how they played.

Longfellow sits deserted tonight because it's just a grass field and a playground. There are no restrooms or restaurants. Not a single adult is available to make teams, keep score, and enforce the rules of the game. There are no coaches or clinicians to teach kids the "proper" way to throw, catch, hit, pass, shoot, and score. Spurred on by Roone Arledge, we've embarked on a journey to span the globe to bring our child a constant variety of sport, the thrill of victory, the agony of defeat, and the human drama of athletic competition. Aside from the actual age of the participants, youth sports has little to do with youth anymore.

The games of my childhood are dead.

My Boy

It's a sunny day in March 1991 and my newly pregnant wife and I are sitting in Dr. Sung's office awaiting the results of our first ultrasound. Because we never had an ultrasound with our first child, this is pretty exciting territory for us. We're both looking forward to taking home pictures of our blurry little baby and sharing them with friends and family. And we've both decided that we'd like to know the sex of the baby in advance.

Dr. Sung hustles into her office and says, "Good news! You have a very healthy baby!" As we look at several slides of the ultrasound, Dr. Sung points out various body organs and limbs and talks about how healthy and well-formed they are. Then she points to a big blob between the baby's legs and says, "You are carrying a healthy baby boy."

"Huh? Are you sure?" I asked. Dr. Sung pointed once again to the big blob and said,

"Oh yes. Very sure. It's a boy."

I was stunned. For three months, I'd been telling anyone who would listen that the gender of our new baby didn't matter to me. Suddenly, all that sensitive male I-don't-care-if-it's-a-boy-or-a-girl rhetoric that I'd been spouting immediately flew out the window. A boy. We had a beautiful five-year-old little girl and now we were expecting a boy. Except it wasn't just "a boy" anymore. All of the sudden, "our baby" had turned into "my boy." As in:

That's my boy.

My son.

My buddy.

Only three months in the womb and I already had my own organic version of the theme from Superman running around in my head. Who can dribble a soccer ball through a herd of helpless defenders? Who can leap four feet in the air to catch the winning touchdown? Who can smack a 460-foot line shot over the Green Monster at Fenway that shatters the Citgo sign into a million pieces?

My boy.

He came into the world kicking and screaming at 8:37p.m. on July 18th. It was 93 degrees outside, the hottest day of 1991. He arrived on his own terms, almost five weeks early after what seemed like 267 hours of labor. Shortly after he was born, Molly arrived at the hospital to see her new baby brother. I remember standing at the window to the hospital nursery with my arms around Molly, both of us looking in at a still-screaming Timothy Zachary Hirschbeck. My beautiful wife was safe and resting comfortably down the hall. I was 28 years old and all of my dreams had already come true.

So it was time to pursue new dreams. After more than a few late-night discussions, it was decided that my wife would remain at her job and I'd stay home to start a new business and take care of the kids. Looking back, it was one of the most exciting and exhausting times of my life. Every day presented a new set of challenges and rewards.

On Molly's first day of kindergarten, I remember hanging out at her bus stop with a dozen other moms and their kids. Word had spread through the neighborhood that I was staying at home with the kids, and it was clear that everyone at the bus stop was curious to see if there was something wrong with me. Most of the moms were very nice, but I got the distinct impression that some of them thought I needed a testosterone transplant.

After I got my daughter on the bus, a very sincere woman in funky Birkenstock sandals approached me and said, "I just want you to know that I think what you're doing is great. Most men wouldn't stay home to baby-sit their children." Though she had good intentions, there was something about that mom's compliment that really bothered me. I wasn't staying home to *baby-sit* my kids. I was their father.

Staying home with Zac opened my eyes to the uneasy truce that many men and women have with the concept of fatherhood. It's a truce that is often reflected in prime-time television. While strong mothers seem to be an essential part of any sitcom or drama, strong fathers apparently don't make good television. TV dads generally fall into one of three categories: First, meet "Ghost Dad." He's the guy that either skipped town, passed away or mysteriously disappeared. Then there's "Sensitive Doormat Dad." He's the guy whose precocious children walk all over him while he stands around in the kitchen making speeches about how much he loves everyone. Finally, there's "Misguided Dad." He's the hardworking guy who thinks he's the head of the household but (wink, wink) we know who *really* wears the pants in the family.

There was a time not too long ago when fatherhood was one of the cornerstones upon which our families rested. Today, we live in the age of the Disposable Dad. If you have a father hanging around the house, that's good. If you don't have a dad, don't worry. A mom, boyfriend, girlfriend, aunt or uncle can all take the place of a father.

No one could ever take my place in the lives of my children. I'm sure someone else could take Zac to Sabres games or help Molly select a college, but I'm their father. My presence in our home teaches our kids hundreds of subtle but essential lessons about life: How a man treats a woman. How a husband honors his marriage. How a father cares for his children. How a son loves his mom.

How to be a man.

In the United States, over 40 percent of our children will go to bed tonight in homes without fathers. Many experts believe that within the next decade, over 60 percent of our nation's children will grow up in homes without dads. American fathers are abandoning their children in droves and no one seems to care.

Except our children. A child without a father faces a future laced with sociological land mines. Children who grow up in homes without dads are far more likely to drop out of school, develop emotional problems, fall victim to child abuse or become absentee parents themselves. Boys with absentee fathers are much more likely to commit violent crimes. In the United States, men who grew up in homes without fathers currently represent over 70 percent of the prison population serving long-term or life sentences.

Zac will turn 13 this July and I'm just starting to come to grips with the fact that he is no longer a little boy. The smell of sweat and dirt has long since replaced that fuzzy baby smell, and his desire to play ball is matched only by his desire to eat everything in our refrigerator. He's a young man now, but he is still my buddy. When I check in on him each night after he falls asleep, I still feel connected to the hottest day of the year back in 1991.

It's a dangerous world that Zac is growing up in, and sometimes it's hard to find ways to deal with its darkness and evil. I'm not a big fan of the symbolic gesture. Hard work and long-term commitment will always solve more problems than a bouquet of flowers or a lighted candle. One of the best ways that I can bring a little light and goodness into the world is to wake up every morning and honor my commitments as a husband and a father.

And to teach my son to do the same.

Mrs. Menas

Fifth grade was a very tough year for my daughter—her toughest year of school in her young life. None of her friends were placed in her classroom. For most of the school year, she struggled with severe stomach problems that were eventually diagnosed as Crohn's Disease. And for the first time, Molly struggled to establish a positive relationship with her teacher.

For the first decade of her life, Molly's relationships with her teachers varied from respect for Mrs. Drake to admiration for Mrs. Gallo to a strong desire to leave our home and be adopted by Mrs. Roaldi. In addition to learning a lot from her teachers, Molly always looked forward to walking into their classrooms each morning.

That all changed in the fifth grade.

Things started in late August when we received notification in the mail that Molly had been placed in the classroom of Mrs. Mean and Nasty (hereafter referred to as Mrs. Menas). Though Molly didn't have any firsthand experience with Mrs. Menas, she had heard rumors that her new teacher possessed a quick temper and yelled a lot in class. My wife and I assured our daughter that these rumors were either greatly exaggerated or completely false. We urged her to ignore all the gossip and make her own judgments. Most importantly, we reminded Molly that she possessed the intelligence, maturity, and work ethic to thrive in any classroom.

Shortly after school began, Molly started to come home each day with a Mrs. Menas story. One day, Mrs. Menas allegedly made a disparaging comment to all the girls in class. On another day, Molly felt she picked on a boy in class. We gave each Mrs. Menas story the attention it deserved, which was not much. After each story, we'd change the subject or offer no comment at all. When Molly pressed the issue, we'd always support both Mrs. Menas and Molly at the same time. The general messages we conveyed to our daughter were: different teachers have different teaching styles; if Molly spent time assembling a daily evaluation of Mrs. Menas, she wasn't spending enough time studying, and the person most responsible for the success or failure of Molly Hirschbeck in Mrs. Menas's classroom was Molly Hirschbeck.

We were happy to find that the messages worked. The Mrs. Menas stories stopped. Molly settled down and brought home excellent grades. Because she didn't have ample opportunity to socialize with her best friends in class or bring in apples for her teacher, Molly focused almost exclusively on her schoolwork. Having a strict albeit slightly nutty teacher was helping Molly to become a better student.

It would be nice if the story ended right there, but unfortunately, it doesn't. Because when Molly's fellow classmates went home to their parents and told them their own Mrs. Menas stories, the reactions of many of their parents were altogether different from ours. Some marched down to school and demanded that their children be placed in another classroom. Many of them contacted other parents to gossip and share their own Mrs. Menas stories. Others repeatedly voiced their displeasure with Mrs. Menas and with the way "the situation was being handled."

All of this in full view of their children.

Dozens of implicit and explicit messages were sent to the students in Mrs. Menas's classroom. The most dangerous centered on three basic ideas:

Mrs. Menas is a horrible teacher.

If you think Mrs. Menas screws up, tell your parents immediately and they will believe every word you say.

The person most responsible for the success or failure of a student in Mrs. Menas's classroom is Mrs. Menas.

It doesn't take a brain surgeon to figure out what happened next. With her students empowered beyond all reasonable limits and without the support of parents, Mrs. Menas slowly began to lose control of the classroom. By spring recess, her students were openly challenging her authority and telling her, "My mom says I don't have to listen to you." By May, the school principal was meeting with the class to listen to their complaints and discuss their behavior in class. In June, a parent asked me if I'd be interested in attending a meeting to demand Mrs. Menas's termination.

Amidst all of this junk, and amidst a handful of health issues that I wouldn't wish on my worst enemy, Molly Hirschbeck went to school each day and treated her teacher with respect and dignity. With minimal amounts of complaints or finger-pointing, she studied hard, got along well with her classmates, and learned a lot about forming her own opinions. She conducted herself with grace and independence. It has been said that nothing shapes an individual's character more than adversity. Without a doubt, Molly learned more life lessons in school during the fifth grade than in all her other 17 years of school combined:

She learned that there are always positive lessons to be taken away from negative experiences.

She learned that the decisive factor as to whether she earns good grades or poor grades is Molly.

She learned that only negative results occur from making excuses for yourself and that only positive results occur from giving your best effort in an activity.

She learned that some authority figures (teachers, police officers, clergy, grandparents, etc.) are deserving of our respect regardless of their shortcomings.

She learned to appreciate the value of hard work and good behavior.

She learned to work with teachers she doesn't particularly care for and has a greater appreciation for individuals she perceives as good teachers.

A few days after the school year concluded, I sat down with Molly to tell her most of the things that I've just shared on these pages. She had lost 30 pounds over the course of the school year and would soon see the inside of a surgical ward for the first time. I wanted to tell my daughter how much I loved her and how proud I was to be her dad. I wanted to tell her that while her future was uncertain and scary, she possessed more character and determination than any other kid I'd ever met.

Towards the end of our conversation, I could tell that she was dying to hear me finally say something critical about Mrs. Menas. To her great disappointment, my only comment was still "no comment." My own personal feelings about Mrs. Menas weren't at issue. They never were. To support my view, I asked Molly if most of the problems in her classroom during the year would have occurred if there were 25 Molly Hirschbecks in Mrs. Menas's classroom. Her reply was "No, I don't think so."

Then I asked if most of the problems would have occurred if the parents in class had offered their children the same type of support as we had offered to her. Again, her reply was "no."

The lesson we learned was that a successful classroom is comprised of three essential components: strong teachers, dedicated students, and supportive parents. The system breaks down when one group tries to abdicate its responsibilities, or assume the role of another. Before anyone rushes down to a school and demands that a teacher be terminated, I'd suggest that person take a long look in the mirror and an honest look at his or her child. The only time anyone will catch me offering a critical opinion of a teacher is if I think that the parents and children in a classroom have exhausted all efforts to create and maintain a constructive classroom.

And if I ever offer criticism, you can bet that I won't do it in front of my kids.

Looking back, it would have been easy to indulge Molly's complaints about Mrs. Menas in the first half of the school year. We would have been heroes if we had mocked her teacher or requested that she be transferred to another classroom. Instead, we offered her our love and support without compromising the respect she had for an authority figure. Giving her our love was easy, but the support didn't come without a hefty amount of self-control and discipline.

One thing I've learned in over 30 years of teaching and coaching young children is that children are usually a reflection of their home environments. The greatest reward that my wife and I receive on a daily basis comes from watching Molly and her brother, Zac, conduct their young lives with love, honesty, discipline, and sensitivity to the needs and feelings of other individuals.

On the other hand, it is sad and more than a little disconcerting to think that Mrs. Menas's classroom frequently resembled a taping of a really bad reality TV show. Honor and respect displaced by a truckload of noise, finger-pointing, and ignorant behavior. In the end, children live what they learn.

My Big Blunder

Ryan Kunz was a bright and talented young guy who played on a basketball team I coached back in the early 90s. He was the kind of kid that every coach loves to have on his team; aggressive, intelligent, cooperative, and absolutely fearless. He also liked girls—a lot.

One of the biggest coaching mistakes that I've ever made occurred on a bitterly cold Saturday morning in January 1993. That morning, Ryan's brain was preoccupied with a pretty little freckle-faced girl on our team named Monica. It was a classic youth-sports love story filled with beauty and betrayal. Ryan was madly in love with Monica, but Monica only had eyes for basketball.

Though it was clear that Ryan's love for his teammate was unrequited, it seemed only to make him try harder to earn her affection. Whenever I stopped practice to give the team instructions, Ryan saw it as an ideal time to chat up Monica.

As a big fan of true love and no stranger to rejection from cute girls, I tried to overlook the whole *As the Kunz Turns* soap opera playing out before my eyes. Eventually, my tolerance reached its end. Ryan was disrupting the team and annoying the heck out of Monica. I asked him to listen once, asked him again, and when he still continued to try to dazzle Monica with his kooky sense of humor, I sat Mr. Kunz off to the sidelines, away from the group.

Practice continues and things are going great. We're playing a passing game called Knockout and all the kids are into it. Everyone is having fun and making big strides in their ability to pass and show an open target for a pass from a teammate. Life is good.

We then start a regular game and things get even better. Most of the players are transferring the lesson to the game. We're seeing tons of passing and for the first time, the kids are looking for a second or third option to pass to instead of passing to the teammate that is closest to them. The parents on the sidelines are going crazy. It's three weeks into the season and these eight- and nine-year-old kids are playing like 12-year-olds.

Halftime rolls around and as I go to my backpack to get a quick slurp from my water bottle, I am pumped. Any good coach I've ever met feels the same way when their players take a big jump up in their skill level. You don't just feel like a good coach, you feel like a magician.

We're about to start the second half of the game when one of the dads quietly approaches me from the sidelines. "What about Ryan?" he whispers. "He's been sitting there for a long time." For a second, I didn't understand his question. Then it hits me...

Ryan!

I had completely forgotten about him. After a quick, discreet glance up at the clock, I try to do the math. My best guess is that Ryan had been sitting on the sidelines for 45 minutes. Why didn't he say anything? Was I that much of a monster that he couldn't approach me and say, "Excuse me coach, I've been sitting on the floor for almost an hour and my butt has been completely numb for the past 20 minutes. Any chance that I could play some basketball today?"

When I sat next to him, Ryan's predicament didn't seem to bother him nearly as much as it bothered me. I apologized a few dozen times, but he just shrugged his shoulders. It was no big deal to him. Maybe he was still thinking warm, fuzzy thoughts about Monica or maybe he just liked being a spectator.

As I guided him back to his team, I remembered that there was someone else who needed an apology. "Are your parents here?" I asked. Ryan explained that his dad was out to breakfast with Ryan's little sister. I told him that I absolutely needed to speak to his dad before he went home.

The game ends and I make a beeline for Mr. Kunz. It's what a friend of mine calls Spill Your Guts Time. No excuses and no explanations; own your mistakes and apologize for them. I tell Ryan's dad the complete story and note that there is no excuse for overlooking a child in class. I apologize for my error and offer to arrange for a full refund for the class.

It was hard to read Mr. Kunz. He obviously wasn't pleased, but it didn't look like he was balling up his fist to take a swing at me, either. Instead, he put a hand on his son's shoulder and said, "There's no need for a refund, Coach Tim. Everyone makes mistakes."

And then Mr. Kunz did something that made me want to give the guy a hug. He gave Ryan's shoulder a squeeze and said, "If Ryan hadn't been talking when his coach was talking, none of this would've happened in the first place. Isn't that right, bud?"

Many parents would have jumped at the opportunity to be a hero in front of their son, to sternly reprimand the big, bad coach in an effort to score some points with their boy. Mr. Kunz wasn't interested in scoring points or heroics—frankly, I don't think he was interested in my apologies.

The only thing that seemed to matter to Mr. Kunz was his son. What could Ryan learn from his coach's error? Should his son assume any responsibility for the problem? What sort of impact did my mistake have on Ryan and what was the likelihood that I'd make the same mistake again in the future?

Mr. Kunz's response to my error turned my biggest coaching blunder into a learning experience for his son. I'll always be thankful for that. He must be in his early 20s today, but I'll bet Ryan is thankful, too.

Fumblebum

When I was a kid, one of my favorite games to play was called Fumblebum. Known in some circles as Fumbly Wumbly or Kill the Guy With the Ball, the game was a perfect mix of athleticism, intelligence, and pure unadulterated mayhem.

The rules of Fumblebum were simple. We'd gather a bunch of guys from around the neighborhood and mark off some space on the grass with our shirts and jackets. The game would begin when one of us threw a football up in the air. Whoever caught the ball would run with it until one (or all) of the other guys tackled him. Once a guy was tackled, he'd purposefully fumble the ball and someone else would pick it up and run until he got tackled. The game would conclude when the streetlights went on or when one of us was loaded by stretcher into an ambulance.

Running around while a bunch of screaming, drooling maniacs try to wrestle you to the ground sounds more like a description of a horror movie than a children's game. Yet the screaming, drooling, and wrestling was the primary appeal of Fumblebum. It provided an excellent opportunity to blow off some steam after a long day in school. Complete your math homework or try to make an open-field tackle on Fumblebum legend Larry "The Lump" Bensen? It was an easy call.

Standing 5'1" and weighing a few dozen donuts over 200 pounds, Larry Bensen was the greatest Fumblebum player of my generation. He was built like a washing machine, an 11-year-old chunk of granite with a bad attitude. I'll never forget the hot

September Saturday afternoon in 1973 when Tommy O'Brien made the mistake of calling Larry a fat pig. Tears welling up in his eyes, Larry stomped and stumbled around Crosby Field for over an hour without getting tackled. It took 15 guys, two Kenmore policemen, the Town of Tonawanda game warden, and a dart gun to finally bring The Lump down that day.

It's funny, Larry was really good at the games we played around our neighborhood but he stunk at playing organized sports. If we were playing Kick the Can or Capture the Flag, The Lump was always a first-round draft pick. Yet when it came to playing in a local baseball or football league, Larry was usually the first guy cut from the team. He never seemed to have the type of skills and temperament that would catch the eye of the dads that coached in our local youth leagues. Larry once said that the thing he liked best about Fumblebum was that there weren't any parents hanging around on the sidelines.

I'm with you, Lump. For me, the best part of Fumblebum was that the game was always ours. If we had let our parents hang around and watch our games, they would have given lectures to the kids who tackled too hard and demanded that we all wear protective equipment. Pretty soon, mom and dad would have created the Kenmore Youth Fumblebum League, organized Fumblebum tournaments and forced us to sell candy bars to pay for our Fumblebum uniforms. Back in 1973, the last thing we needed was a bunch of goofy adults messing up a good thing.

Kids don't play Fumblebum anymore. The games that my friends and I played and loved as kids have been replaced by highly structured organized-sports programs. Fumblebum and Capture the Flag are on the brink of extinction, cast aside by soccer domes and baseball academies. In other words, a bunch of goofy adults have messed up a good thing.

When I was younger, I'd often wonder if I was messing up a good thing for my own son. Though there were things that Zac could do on a ball field that would leave me shaking my head in disbelief, I noticed that he didn't smile or laugh much when he played ball. It was hard to tell if he liked to play because he was good at it or because he truly loved the game. I wondered if, 30 years down the road, he'd look back on his travel soccer league as fondly as I look back on Fumblebum.

When he was eight years old, I showed Zac and a bunch of his friends how to play Fumblebum. It was the day before Columbus Day, a rainy and windy Sunday afternoon tailor-made for a couple of hours of Fumbly Wumbly. Within 10 minutes of starting the game, the boys were covered in mud and piling on top of each other with reckless abandon. By the end of the afternoon, some of the guys were doing full-fledged belly flops into giant mud puddles. Later that night, I received two calls from parents who weren't too thrilled at having their sons arrive home dripping in mud.

The Lump would have been proud.

Copenhagen

Twenty years and two weeks ago, my wife and I traveled to Denmark for our honeymoon. We were young, poor, and completely unprepared for the country that awaited us on the other side of the ocean. With little money for transportation, we spent most of our time walking hand in hand through the streets of Copenhagen. We explored every castle, garden, art gallery, bookstore, and bakery within a 10-mile radius of our hotel. Our diet consisted of chocolate, wine, cheese, bread, and more chocolate. It was the perfect way for a newly married couple to begin their life together.

One of the first things I noticed on our long walks together was that, compared to Americans, Europeans had a very different perspective on youth sports. Back in the United States, youth sports was gradually turning into big business. Children were playing soccer in domes equipped with artificial turf and state-of-the-art scoreboards. In my hometown, eight-year-old baseball players were playing night games under the lights on finely manicured diamonds. The facility in which a child played and what he or she wore while playing had suddenly become more important than the game itself.

In the early 1980s, a strange sort of class warfare crept into youth sports. Playing sports was no longer something that all of the kids in a neighborhood could do together. Adults had created new classifications for players. Playing on a "house" league team was OK, a "travel" team was better, while an invitation to an "elite" or "select" team was the youth sports equivalent of admission to an Ivy League school.

Things were very different in Denmark. Every courtyard, parking lot, and public park hosted a group of children playing soccer and every game seemed to have flexible rules and structure. Some games consisted of five kids kicking a can around in a narrow cobblestone alley while other games involved a swarm of 40 kids playing with a tattered ball in a school courtyard. No one wore uniforms but everyone seemed to know who was on their team. There were no age or gender restrictions. Most of the games that I saw involved teenagers playing side by side with first graders.

Play was friendly but intense. While I can't say that I saw anyone play dirty, it was a much more physical brand of youth soccer than I had ever seen. The skill of the kids was unbelievable. I was amazed at the creativity and dribbling—even the youngest players seemed to have the ball on a string.

It took a few days for me to recognize the most significant difference between youth sports in Europe and the United States: there were no adults. We must have wandered past a few dozen soccer matches during our honeymoon and in all that time, I didn't see a single adult hovering over the kids. There were no coaches, instructors, or referees. None of the kids needed a mom or dad to transport them to the game, form teams, or make sure that everyone played fair. As far as I could tell, the kids assumed all of those responsibilities all by themselves.

I'm not sure what parents in Copenhagen did with their free time—many of the men seemed particularly fond of public intoxication—but it was clear that adults had no particular interest in the scores of their seven-year-olds' soccer games. Back in the United States, parents were starting to live their lives through their kids. In Denmark, parents were still living lives of their own.

Sportswriters and pundits often wonder aloud why the United States gets its ass kicked in the World Cup every four years. Decade after decade, we get beat by perennial superpowers like Ecuador, Turkey, and Iran. How do tiny countries with a fraction of our population and resources stomp all over our soccer team?

There is no simple answer to that question, but a big part of the problem may be the way in which our young athletes are introduced to soccer. In every other corner of the world, children discover soccer in unstructured settings on streets, playgrounds, and parking lots. They learn the game from older siblings and friends. Soccer is filled with freedom, fun, and friendship. It is a game that can be played from age three to age 93.

In the United States, children have been introduced to soccer in the same way for the past 30 years. Their first exposure to the game is through highly structured programs where, at the ages of five and six, they are taught by adults who demand that they stay restricted to positions and adhere to an extensive list of rules. Playing soccer is a regimented activity. It is a game that is discarded by the vast majority of American youth by the time they reach middle school.

The best soccer player I've coached over the past three decades was a 10-year-old boy named Vandi. In many respects, he reminded me of the kids I saw in Denmark— only he was five times more talented. Vandi is the only player I've met who could conceivably take on a team of five or six players and beat them single-handedly.

Vandi didn't develop his freakish talent on a select team in Virginia or at an Olympic Development Program in Florida. He came to the United States from Sierra Leone. For those unfamiliar with that part of the world, imagine a land in which 98 percent of its citizens live in abject poverty, throw in some of the most horrendous human rights violations that have occurred on this planet in the past century, and you've got Sierra Leone. Vandi had been adopted by a wonderful family in my hometown. His parents and all of his brothers and sisters had been murdered.

How does a kid who has grown up in hell on earth possess such breathtaking soccer skills? The simplest answer is that he played—a lot. With friends, with neighbors, but mostly by himself. No coaches, no scoreboard, no travel teams, and, other than a beat-up ball donated by a world relief organization, no equipment. We've all heard the expression "he played as if his life depended on it." Most of the time, that expression is casually used to describe professional athletes who live in the lap of luxury. In Vandi's case, he really did play soccer as if his life depended on it. His game was filled with desperation, creativity, and love.

There is a lesson to be learned here by anyone who coaches young athletes. It is easy to get caught up in teaching our players skills, tactics, and theory, but our primary goal as youth coaches should be to foster a love of the game. Often, that requires us to do something that makes American coaches and parents very uncomfortable: we must quietly move to the sidelines and let our kids have the freedom to create, make mistakes, and compete.

The game must always belong to children.

Bobby

It's the first night of the summer season and my head is spinning. Even though I've been working with kids for 60 kazillion years, the first night of a soccer league is always hectic. Practice starts in 20 minutes and I've got a hundred things to do before the kids arrive to the field. I'm marking the field with some cones when a mom approaches me and asks if she can talk to me about her son, Bobby. Before I can reply, Bobby's mom tells me the following:

"Bobby has been classified as functional autistic. He can hear what you're saying but he won't always respond. We're playing around with his medication right now—it tends to make him very irritable. He's also very sensitive to the sun and we're pretty sure he has exercise-induced asthma. Oh, and Bobby's very allergic to bee stings! If he gets stung, we need to get him to the hospital immediately."

Practice is scheduled to start in seven minutes and the synapses in my head are shorting out. My brain is making sounds that remind me of one of those big, blue electric bug zappers in the front of a 7 Eleven. Functional autistic? What kind of medication is he on and why does it make him irritable? Exercise-induced asthma? Does Bobby have an inhaler or am I just supposed to wing it if he starts gasping for air? Will you be rushing him to an emergency room if a bee stings him or should we just dial 911?

What I wanted to say to Bobby's mom was this:

"Let me get this straight, your little boy can't follow instructions, can't run 15 yards without wheezing, views the sun as his mortal enemy, and

shrieks like a fire engine whenever there is a bee, mosquito or flying ant within 10 feet of him? Welcome to soccer! I bet he'll really enjoy learning to play a game in which players must listen, cooperate with their teammates, run a lot, and remain in close proximity to sunshine, mosquitoes, and bumble bees at all times. Ever hear the story about the square peg and the round hole?"

What I actually said was this:

"OK, thanks for the info. I'll do the best I can."

I definitely wanted to help Bobby in any way that I could. He was a cute little guy and my heart went out to him and his mom. Over the years, I'd generally had a good deal of success coaching kids with special needs. I was hopeful that playing soccer could be a great experience for Bobby.

At the end of practice, I was a lot less hopeful. Whenever the ball came close to him, Bobby would pounce on it like a squirrel and pick it up with his hands. He was overtly physical with some of the kids—pushing and grabbing seemed to be his primary way of communicating with others. Though his fear of bees was understandable, it was also totally disruptive. At least four or five times that night, Bobby thought he saw a bee and ran squealing to his mom.

As the weeks passed, we made some serious progress with Bobby. A friend of mine who worked as a special education teacher was able to give our coaches some guidance on working with autistic kids, guidance that we weren't getting from Bobby's mom. We progressed to the point where Bobby would refrain from snatching the ball up into his arms, but not to where he wasn't extremely disruptive to the rest of the kids. He still grabbed and pushed other players; he still ran wailing to his mom several times a night; and he had very little interest in actually playing soccer.

The beginning of the end came during the sixth week of the season. Bobby was supposed to be playing goalie, but he was more interested in chasing after a girl on the other team. Something about this little girl captivated Bobby's attention that night, and he was intent on standing a few inches away from her face. Having her personal space regularly invaded—probably for the first time in her life—freaked out the little girl and she ran crying to the sidelines.

To her credit, Bobby's mom came out on the field to stand next to him in an effort to keep him connected to playing goalie, but Bobby had no interest in soccer or mom. Once the little girl on the other team began to cry, he became even more transfixed on her.

So imagine the scene. The little girl is screeching into her dad's shoulder as Bobby tries to get her attention. Bobby's 30-something mom is showing great lateral quickness in playing goalie for his team. The little girl's dad is wondering if he should run off into the car and head home for the night or tell the unusual little boy standing next to him to back the hell away from his kid. Bobby's mom is yelling to her son to join her in net while two of my fellow coaches and I are quickly trying to extinguish all of these fires. There are 21 other seven- and eight-year-old players at the game, all of whom have needs of their own, and their coaches are completely ignoring them because all of their attention is fixed on the boy who is afraid of bees.

After the game, I spoke with Bobby's mom and told her that I didn't think our league was a proper fit for her son. I told her that I didn't have the necessary training and experience to work effectively with Bobby, and I expressed the concern that her son's needs were taking instructional time away from all the other players in the league.

I felt as though I was stating the obvious and expected that Bobby's mom would understand my concerns. It would be an understatement to say she didn't. Right from the start, she said, none of the coaches in the league liked Bobby. She told me that her son had just as much of a right to play soccer as all of the other kids.

I noted that she had played more soccer that night than Bobby and that it didn't work to have 30-year-old moms playing against eight-year-old kids. While I understood her desire to integrate Bobby into traditional activities with other kids, I told her that it seemed like Bobby hated playing soccer.

She reiterated that I had a problem with her son and suggested that I didn't like any kid who wasn't "normal." As she stomped over to the playground to collect Bobby, she told me that she and her husband would be speaking to a lawyer. Her last words to me were "You'll be hearing from me soon. This isn't over."

For a few months, I sorted through the daily mail expecting to find an angry lawyer letter from Bobby's mom, but I never heard from her again.

Mainstreaming special needs students into regular classrooms has become a common practice in public school systems across America, and with good reason. Educating kids with physical and developmental disabilities alongside non-disabled kids can foster understanding and tolerance, two values that are in increasingly short supply in our culture.

According to my friend the special education teacher, mainstreaming can be particularly beneficial for students with autism. Because children with autism often possess severely restricted interests and weak communication skills, the increased interaction with students in the general school population can be of great help to them.

For all its benefits, the road to a mainstreamed classroom has been filled with a number of potholes. Parents of "regular" students have complained that placing a student with a significant disability into a traditional classroom draws resources and instruction away from the majority of students. Some parents of special needs students have advocated for the total elimination of special education classrooms; others have fought to preserve them; while still others have argued that a hybrid schedule of mainstreamed classes and special education classes is the ideal solution.

Years later, I still wonder if I could have handled things differently and somehow connected with Bobby. Though his mother's threats and unreasonable expectations led me to want to push her off the nearest steep cliff, it still feels like I failed Bobby. With a few years of hindsight, here is an alternate path I wish we could have taken:

My biggest wish is that Bobby's mom would have contacted me a few weeks before the start of the season to talk about his disability. It would have helped to have had some history of his experiences in other group activities, and I would have liked to have been able to ask some of the questions that were spinning around in my head when his mom approached me on the first night of the league. The more information I have about a child—especially a child with special needs—the greater the chance that I can do effective work with the child.

Bobby's mom gave me an extensive list of diagnoses and symptoms that applied to her son, but she offered no practical guidance or help. Did he respond well to specific words or phrases? Would it help to adjust my tone or phrasing? Could he follow authoritative, full-group instruction or should all of my instruction be quiet and conversational? It felt like Bobby's mom was tying my arms and legs to a chair and expecting me to figure out how to dance.

Bobby's mom seemed entrenched in the position that her son's disability should not limit him in any way. That's a pleasant thought, but it's not particularly realistic. Inevitably, a disability takes away some options. It felt like the mom believed that we could turn Bobby into a soccer player by the sheer force of our will. In her mind, any result that fell short of that goal was failure.

Looking back, both of us wanted Bobby to have a successful experience playing team sports, but from the beginning, it felt like we were adversaries instead of two people who shared a common goal. I let my frustration with the mom steer me away from communicating with her, and she clearly had no interest in talking to me. I wish both of us would have recognized that whether we liked it or not, we were partners.

The Seven Demandments

Although my wife and I are probably a bit more strict with our kids than the average parent, neither of us are devotees of Miss Manners. More often than not, our children forget to pick up their rooms, watch too much television, and go to school with traces of breakfast scattered about their face and clothing. Yet if you met Molly or Zac at a party, words like "respectful" and "courteous" might come to mind.

Our secret to raising well-mannered children has been moderation and discipline. In other words, Tricia and I have tried to select a few manners and principles that are most important to us and insist that the kids adhere to them. What follows is a list of manners that are most important around our house. Our kids affectionately (or maybe it's sarcastically, it's hard to tell at their age) refer to them as the "The Seven Demandments."

Demandment 1 "I won't repeat myself."

Indifference is probably the most common form of disrespect that children display toward adults. A couple of years ago, Tricia and I were going crazy. Every statement or request that we made to the kids was greeted with a blank stare and a "Huuhh?"

After tearing our hair out for a while, we made the decision that we would not repeat ourselves anymore. If we spoke to the kids and they said "Huh?" we'd calmly reply, "I'm not going to repeat myself" and walk away. At the end of the day, we'd tell the kids what they missed. "I asked you earlier if you wanted to invite your friend over for a sleepover. It's too bad you didn't hear me." or "I asked you to load the dishwasher earlier. Apparently, you didn't hear me because I had to load the dishwasher myself and now I have no choice but to take away TV privileges tonight." Within 48 hours, the kids miraculously started to hear everything we said to them. Selective deafness cured.

Demandment 2 "Ummmphh, uh huh, or other assorted grunts and groans are not an answer."

This is a big one. Grunting and mumbling is a convenient way for children to be rude and insolent to adults. Tricia and I don't insist that our kids use perfect grammar when they speak, but we always insist that they converse in actual words. In our house, "Yes" is always better than "Uh huh" and "No" is always better than "Mmmpphhhh."

Demandment 3 "If you don't have anything interesting to contribute to a conversation, be quiet."

I've never subscribed to the idea that children should be seen and not heard, but I do believe that if children are going to be heard, they should speak clearly and have something interesting to say. Molly understands that silence is a positive alternative to telling us a story that is chock full of "like," "and I go," and "uh." At the tender age of five, Zac understood that when Grandma was talking about her childhood, it was not a good time to initiate a conversation about his favorite NHL goalie.

Demandment 4 "Don't take that tone with me."

As soon as Molly turned seven, she developed the unique ability to say the same word one thousand different ways. Just a simple "OK" could mean anything from "I will love you forever, mom and dad" to "You guys are scum and at this very moment, I'm hatching a plot to poison your breakfast cereal, send Zac to an orphanage, and run away to New York City to pursue a career as a runway model." When it comes to expressing yourself clearly, tone is just as important as words.

Demandment 5 "Chew with your mouth closed"

Is there anything more disgusting than sitting across a table from a seven-year-old eating a piece of pizza and being forced to view the Jackson Pollock painting inside his mouth? If the view isn't sickening enough, just the sound of a child chomping on their food can send me on an emergency flight to the nearest rest room. The general rule in our house is that once the kids were old enough to use a knife and fork, they were old enough to chew their food with their mouths closed.

Demandment 6 "Respect your elders"

Few things make me bristle more than children who are allowed to treat anyone over the age of 60 like they are senile, a piece of furniture or servants. Let's not ignore reality: old people generally dress, speak, and behave differently than the rest of us. This gives parents an ideal vehicle to teach their kids to recognize and embrace individual differences (i.e., "Grandpa sticks french fries up his nose because he loves you and likes to make you laugh. Just smile and remember that he's your Grandpa.").

Instead of taking advantage of the opportunity, many parents regress back to high school, mocking and snickering at an elder's dress and behavior behind their back. How can parents expect their child to treat them with love and respect if they don't treat their own mom and dad in the same manner?

Demandment 7 "Don't interrupt me"

Television and radio don't help parents much in conveying this idea to our children. Interrupting each other has become standard operating procedure in our country. The average political talk show is built around the premise that millions of Americans will tune in to witness grown adults interrupting each other for 30 minutes. The precocious six-year-old that interrupts adult conversations with a sarcastic observation is a staple of television sitcoms.

The implicit message sent to our kids is that interrupting adults is not only acceptable, it's also a cute, funny, and intelligent way of expressing yourself. In our house, medical emergencies, natural disasters, or a breaking news bulletin on ESPN are the only acceptable excuses for interrupting a conversation between two adults.

The Oath

A few weeks ago, my sister-in-law and her husband hopped on a plane and traveled to the other side of the world to adopt a baby girl. On September 16th, Katie Xui Yan became the newest member of our family.

From a distance, I have watched Katie's parents jump through a hundred hoops in order to prove that they are qualified to adopt a child. Home visits, extensive background checks and mandatory parenting workshops are just a few of the steps that they've taken over the past two years in their march to bring home their little girl. It seems to have been an exhausting process.

Which isn't to say that my sister-in-law and her husband are complaining. Far from it. Having their life examined with a fine-tooth comb only served to reaffirm their belief that they were ready to adopt a baby.

Wouldn't the world be a better place if all prospective parents had to subject themselves to the same 720-day cross-examination that adoptive parents are forced to endure? We live in a world where you need a license to catch a fish, shoot a duck, or bring a dog into your home. Why don't you need a license to assume life's greatest responsibility? Forget about Flipper, Daffy, and Rover. We should all have to obtain a license to bring a child into the world.

Of course, there's a big problem with this idea: who is going to issue the license? The government has enough on its plate these days without getting into the baby permit business. Separation of church and state would prevent us from handing the responsibility over to a religious organization. What's needed here is an independent authority figure who loves kids, but is sensitive to the trials and tribulations of parenthood. We need someone with a superior intellect, a receding hairline and a direct line to the soul of Ward and June Cleaver.

I vote for me.

OK, I admit that I'm a bit lacking in the intellect category, but I used to watch *Leave It To Beaver* a lot when I was a kid and let's face it, I'm all over the receding hairline thing.

So here's my idea.

If you want to have a child in America, you must sign and adhere to an Oath of Parenthood. Abide by the Oath for 18 years and the government will pick up 75 percent of the cost of your child's college education (we'll figure out how to pay for stuff later). Violate the terms and conditions of the Oath and your kid's tuition is all on you.

Here's a first draft of the Oath:

We hereby certify that we are a we.

We pledge that before we even considered having a baby, we purchased a dog first. We're proud to say that Milo is still alive. When he threw up on the antique Oriental rug, neither one of us freaked out. When he got a urinary tract infection, we fed him his pills even if it took 20 tries before he finally swallowed. Even when we're sick, stressed or exhausted, we always take Milo for his walk and make sure that he's fed on time.

We certify that we know at least three people that we consider to be excellent parents. We've watched these people mix formula, strap in a car seat, assemble a tricycle, change a diaper, give hugs, apply band-aids, reprimand, punish, visit the emergency room and explain why it's not nice to talk like Uncle Danny. When we have problems raising our child, these are the folks that we'll turn to for advice.

We certify that we don't want to have kids to make up for our own dysfunctional childhoods. We recognize that if we're spending too much time thinking about our past, we're not spending enough time thinking about our baby's present and future.

We pledge to do our best to love our fellow man and to teach our child to do the same. The phrases "their kind", "that type" and "those people" will never pass our lips.

We attest that we are well-rounded adults with a variety of hobbies and interests. Our lives will not revolve around whether or not our child's team wins the Tri-County Junior Soccer League Championships. If our kid fails to be admitted into the Gifted and Talented program, we will not lock ourselves in the closet for a week.

We promise that we will never use the plural possessive when describing our child's activities (as in, 'We lost a heartbreaker in the championship game last night' or 'We really like our new violin teacher'). We will let our child's opinions, interests and accomplishments be his or hers alone.

We certify that we have friends. Adult friends. Once we reached the age of 23, we ceased caring what people under the age of 18 thought about us. We have no interest in being our child's friend. We have every interest in being our child's parent.

We will love each other for better or worse and even when we're going through a rough patch of the very worst, we will never denounce each other in front of our child.

In an effort to keep those patches of the very worst to an absolute minimum, we pledge to go out on a date at least once a month. No cell phones, no toys and no baby talk. Just us. We pledge to remember that before we were a family, we were an us.

We promise to remember that our child is fallible. If a teacher calls and tells us that our child pushed a classmate into a drinking fountain, we will assume that our child actually pushed a classmate into a drinking fountain. For the chances are far greater that our kid got hopped up on one too many juice boxes at lunch and lost self-control than that the 54-year-old teacher is A) a rabid conspiracy theorist who has it in for our child or B) an incompetent jerk who purchased a teaching degree on eBay. Our children will live in fear of having a bad report come home from their teacher. They'll understand that it's their job to work hard in order to please their teachers and not the other way around.

Unless our children are in serious danger or the victim of gross misconduct, we will not fight their battles for them. While we won't be happy when they come home with tears in their eyes, we'll recognize that bruises, hurt feelings and tears are a part of growing up. We understand that a child who never learns to handle adversity will likely remain a child forever.

Our expectations for our child will not change due to the surrounding environment. Just because our child is out in a public place—say, a toy store or over at a friend's house—it will not give him or her license to be a snotty, selfish kid.

In an effort to carry on a family tradition, we pledge to tell our children to eat everything on their plates because there are millions of starving kids in China who would kill for a helping of boiled carrots—and we'll remember that there was always a grain of truth in the weird things that our parents said to us a thousand times.

As soon as our child can pick up their toys or pour a glass of juice, they will do so on a regular basis.

When we do something in public for our children, like coach their baseball team or attend a PTA meeting, we won't expect anyone to throw a parade in our honor. We believe that when a parent donates time to improve the life of a child, it should be selfless act of volunteerism, not part of a competition to see who can be The Parents That Do the Most For Their Child.

We'll remember that the most important part of our job is to be there. If forced to decide between working overtime in order to take yearly trips to Walt Disney World or getting home early so that we can eat dinner together, we'll choose a family dinner even if it's just hot dogs and tater tots.

Finally, we pledge to remember that one of the great universal truths of good parenting is that children live what they learn. Our lives will serve as a living textbook to our child. With that in mind, we promise to kiss in public places, vote, speak clearly, keep an open mind, admit our mistakes, exercise regularly, laugh at ourselves, take risks and express our love for each other every day.

The Price You Pay

We were inching through the Williamsville toll barriers on New Year's Day when I saw one up close for the first time. I glanced over at a minivan next to us and saw two little munchkins gazing up at one of those new portable televisions that pop down from the ceiling.

They could have been an advertisement for a car company, the modern American family enjoying its new automotive theater system. No arguments in the back seat about who hit who first. No threats from the parents to turn the car around and return home if the kids couldn't behave. All eyes in the back seat were perched up at the television and all eyes in the front seat were gazing at the road ahead.

It was one of the saddest things I have ever seen.

My wife practically had to restrain me from jumping out of our car and sprinting over to the minivan. I wanted to leap onto their windshield and tell them that it didn't have to be like this. Surely they could understand that there are more healthy family activities than the 43rd showing of a Wiggles video. The pop-down television might keep the kids under control on the trip home from Grandma's, but at what price?

Make no mistake about it; there is always a price. Any time we accept a new piece of technology into our lives, we give away a tiny piece of our soul. A cell phone might bring us closer to work and a video game system might bring our kids closer to Buzz Lightyear, but that technology inevitably creates distance between us and the most important people in our world.

As a child, I had a real love-hate relationship with family car rides. Placing five young kids and one chain-smoking mother in a '76 Buick Skylark for five hours always had the potential to develop into an explosive situation. I have vivid memories of looking up from the backseat at my mom's face in the rear view mirror, a Pall Mall clenched in her teeth, desperately trying to make everyone in the car behave.

Yet for all the emotional and psychological trauma that a family car ride could inflict on my mom, I think she loved being in that old Buick with all of her kids. For her, one of the best things about a family car ride was that there was no television. Over the previous decade, she had watched the RCA XL-100 AccuColor television in the family room gradually extinguish most of the conversation and creativity that existed in our home. Strapping her kids into a metal box traveling at 60mph forced us to be a family.

Family meant different things to different people in the car. My mother loved to drive out into the country and tell us stories about her childhood. An abandoned barn might trigger a story about a flour mill my grandfather owned and struggled to keep afloat during the Great Depression. Driving over railroad tracks might bring the tale of her first trip to New York City just months after the end of World War II. My mom's childhood always seemed richer and darker than my own, a tapestry of Ku Klux Klan rallies, food rationing, hobos who traveled the country on railroad cars, and kids who set outhouses on fire on Halloween.

To my youngest brother, our car was a family recreation room. On long vacation trips, he'd conduct marathon games of Crazy 8's, Blackjack, and Gin Rummy in the back seat. He loved to make up his own games. "Pick a side of the car," he'd say. "Cows count as one point, gas stations count as five points and horses count as 10. You can only count stuff on your side of the car. Whoever finishes with the most points by the end of the trip owes the other guy a quarter."

My oldest brother had a more sadistic view of what constituted fun in the car. He was never truly happy unless one of his siblings was doubled over in pain. A master of many ancient methods of torture, his favorite weapon was something called "the Spike" which involved making a fist, extending the knuckle of his index finger, and repeatedly punching one of us in the thigh until he heard the crackling of splintered femur or the pain caused us to vomit and lose consciousness.

We were all voracious readers and regularly brought books with us on family trips. It was an unspoken family rule that if something we read made us laugh out loud, we had to read it aloud to everyone else in the car. I think those were my mom's favorite times in that old Buick. She loved the sight of all of her kids, noses pressed in a book, reading their favorite passages aloud to each other.

The last of the Hirschbeck family car rides slowly came to an end in our driveway almost 40 years ago, but the acrid smoke of my mom's Pall Malls still swirls in my nostrils, and the mere thought of the Spike crushing my femoral artery still makes my heart race. What of the two little munchkins in the back of the minivan staring up at their pop-down TV screen? What are the stories they'll tell their kids 40 years down the road?

CETA

When I was six months old, my father left our house and several years later, left town for good. With the benefit of four decades of hindsight, I can see that never meeting my father inevitably brought some significant adversity into my life. Yet if we had the ability to travel back in time and ask the six-, 16-, or 26-year-old versions of me about the absence of my father, I'd happily tell you that I had a life that was pretty close to perfect. However, even at an early age, I remember missing money. Though I'm sure we qualified, my mom never allowed us to collect public assistance. Our family's primary weapon against poverty was work. My mom worked hard and when we were all legally able to do so, she expected that her kids would find work, too.

Throughout most of my childhood, I watched my brothers and my sister trudge home from jobs in steel plants, warehouses, and restaurants. They hated their work. I was fortunate to find a job as a counselor at a YMCA summer camp when I was 14 years old. From the moment I stepped onto a soccer field and started working with kids, I was hooked.

Do you remember that part in *The Grinch Who Stole Christmas* when the Grinch's heart grows so big that it breaks the X-ray machine? That was me on my first day on the job. Placed into a situation where I had to work hard and consider the needs and feelings of someone other than myself, my tiny teenage Grinch heart grew 10 times its normal size that day.

How does a lazy 14-year-old kid with no prior work experience snag a full-time summer camp position at a YMCA? I wish I could tell you that it's because I gave a dazzling interview, but that would be a lie. The truth is that I got hired because the YMCA didn't have to pay my salary.

You paid my salary.

Actually, it was probably your parents who paid me. Anyone who was paying federal income tax between 1978 and 1982 saw a microscopic fraction of their tax dollars go to fund a program called the Comprehensive Employment and Training Act (CETA), a $2 billion jobs initiative designed to, as Congress put it, "provide underprivileged youth with the basic education, training, and work experience they need to compete in the labor market of the 1980s." The arrangement was pretty simple: 1) The YMCA trained, supervised, and treated me just like a regular employee, 2) I worked my butt off, and 3) every taxpayer in the U.S. contributed roughly one ten thousandth of a penny to pay my wages.

At the risk of sounding vain, I think I've given American taxpayers a solid return on their investment. The training I received in the CETA program helped me to be a better coach and, in turn, helped me to give tens of thousands of children a fun and interesting introduction to youth sports. My wife and I have owned a company that, since its inception in 1991, has brought positive energy into dozens of schools in Western New York and employed more than 180 people.

Compared to other CETA alumni, I'm no big success story. There are thousands of people walking around America who have given your parents a far greater return on their investment. There are folks who used CETA as a springboard to start software companies that employ 800 people. Some former CETA employees have used their work experience to build homeless shelters, rehab centers, and soup kitchens.

My guess is that there are also tens of thousands of people that didn't take full advantage of the opportunity that CETA provided them. Still, I'm not sure that it would be fair to classify those folks as a waste of tax dollars. Even if those kids royally messed up, CETA still put food on their table and clothes on their back. If I had turned into a bank robber instead of a coach, do you think your parents would regret spending a fraction of one penny to help my mom raise five kids all on her own?

In 1980, America elected a new president and by 1982, CETA was just one of many programs gutted by the new administration. All of the opportunities that CETA gave to my family and me disappeared. While lots of folks view the 1980s as a time of great economic prosperity, I've always looked at the decade as a time when America lost a little of its heart and soul, a time when it became acceptable—even fashionable—to stop looking out for the guy next to you.

It's scary for me to look back and think about what my life would have been like without your help. If I had been forced to enter the job market without CETA as an option, the YMCA would never have taken a chance on me. With no CETA program to steer me into the joys of teaching young children, I would have likely taken a very different career path. I would never have met my wife, started a family, or summoned the courage to start my own business. Looking back, it's easy to see that the things that I hold closest to my heart all trace their way back to my first job.

Like most Americans, I have to restrain myself from jumping off the nearest cliff when I write out my checks every April 15th. Yet my frustration would be a lot less palpable if I knew my money was going to help restore programs like CETA. I'd happily pay more taxes to fund a national program that trains kids to work as coaches, teachers, and referees in youth sports leagues. How much energy and innovation could we introduce into traditional youth sports programs with a generation of young, enthusiastic, highly trained coaches? How many future leaders would get their start as players and coaches in that type of program? How much leadership, goodwill, and teamwork would come from young athletes and young, professional coaches working side by side?

If a 14-year-old kid is looking to gain valuable job skills and is willing to bust his butt to get those skills, the collective response of our government should be more than a shrug and a lecture about personal responsibility.

Back in 1978, I didn't need lectures and shrugs.

I needed a job.

I needed your help.

Treasure Hunt

My daughter and I don't agree on anything. Which is natural, I guess. She's 14 going on 22 and I'm 37 going on 12, so there isn't exactly a lot of common ground between us. Molly thinks the Backstreet Boys are the next Dylan; I think the Backstreet Boys are the next Duran Duran. I keep up on the day's news by listening to NPR; Molly stays on top of current events by listening to Kiss 98.5. I think I'm a pretty charming and funny guy most of the time; Molly thinks I'm an idiot.

Today, we have discovered a common interest, something that any healthy, red-blooded American father and daughter can enjoy together. The name of that something is Julia Roberts. Molly likes Julia Roberts because she is very skilled at portraying bright, funny women in romantic comedies. I like Julia Roberts because, well, she's Julia Roberts.

Most of our day has been one big Julia Robertsfest. We started our morning watching *Runaway Bride*. Not Julia's best effort, but significant for the fact that she makes a piece of driftwood like Richard Gere almost watchable.

Around lunchtime, we popped *Notting Hill* into the old VCR. We agree that this is a much better effort. Hugh Grant is much more likeable than Richard Snore, the supporting cast is funny, and the film has lots of 90-second close-ups of our beloved Julia just being Julia.

Which brings us to the Stanley Cup of Julia Roberts movies: *My Best Friend's Wedding*. In this rom com, Julia competes with Cameron Diaz (a major bonus) for the affections of some guy that reminds us a lot of Richard Gere. The movie makes my Top 10 List because for most of the second half of the movie, Julia runs around in a baby blue belly shirt that, if there was any justice in the world, would have been placed in the Smithsonian years ago.

It is 3p.m. and Molly and I have spent more time together in one day than we have for the previous month. We have eaten a homemade lunch together and laughed at the same parts of movies. We've talked about her college plans, her teachers, music, her friends, politics, her brother and how much she reminds me of her mom sometimes. She is still my little girl and, at least for a few moments, I am not an idiot.

All is right with the world.

Well, not everything. It would be a lot nicer if we were home. No industrial size fluorescent lights overhead. No strange voices on the other side of the door. No muffled clicking from the machine that delivers 280 milliliters and $3,000 worth of medicine into Molly's right arm.

We come here to Strong Memorial Hospital in Rochester every three or four months. It's a 90-minute trip from our house—longer if it snows and even longer if we stop to pick up donuts for the nurses. The staff here is amazing. Each visit, they set us up in a private room with comfortable reclining chairs, a television with a VCR and a selection of 75 movies. They order us pizza and hand out stuffed animals and let us use the phone (no cell phones in the hospital) whenever we need to. It's almost enough to make us forget we're in a hospital for six hours.

Any serious illness carries its own unique set of pros and cons. Since Molly was diagnosed with Crohn's Disease in 1997, my wife and I have tossed those pros and cons around in our heads a thousand times. Pro: Crohn's isn't terminal. Con: There is no cure for the disease. Pro: For the most part, Molly will be able to lead a normal life. Con: When Crohn's does rear its ugly head, the symptoms can be pretty traumatic. Pro: Effective medication exists to treat the symptoms of Crohn's. Con: The side effects of the medication can be so severe that sometimes we've found ourselves wondering which was worse, the disease or the medication. Amidst all the pros and cons was the overwhelming sense that no kid should have to go through this stuff.

Three years ago, our 5'4" daughter weighed 77 pounds. She'd seen the inside of a surgical ward, been hooked up to a variety of tubes and wires, and was on a first-name basis with the folks at our local pharmacy. While most of her friends were out swimming, riding bikes and going to summer camp, Molly had only enough energy to sleep, read, eat, and sleep some more. She was skin and bones and we were all at the end of our rope.

Or so we thought. Each time we visit the hospital, we see people whose rope appears to be quite a bit longer than ours. Compared to the other patients here on the sixth floor at Strong Memorial, Molly has the equivalent of a rough case of the sniffles. Most of the kids are here for chemotherapy and other assorted blood-related therapies.

Out in the waiting room, we saw a little baby—maybe 18 months old—who breathes out of a tube installed in her trachea. She seemed like a happy baby out in the waiting room, but the faces of her mom and her aunt tell a different story. They are wearing funeral faces, a waxy fatigue that tells the world that you've cried so much that you can't cry anymore. As we pass their room on the way to our appointment, the trach tube is morphing the baby's crying into something that sounds a lot like the whistle of a toy train.

Outside of our room sits a woman with bleach blonde hair, stonewashed jeans and a black Denver Broncos baseball cap pulled down tight over her eyes. She is very young, wears no wedding ring, and apologizes to the nurses a hundred times each time she asks them for help. In her arms rests a tiny little baby, no more than six months old, wearing a floppy blue Gilligan hat. Above her shoulder is a small red bag of blood connected to her baby with two red tubes. When she needs to visit the nurse's station or use the phone, the mom will stay seated in her chair, cradle her baby in her right arm while grasping the IV distributor with her left, brace her feet on the floor, and push off with her legs until her chair slides to the desired location. She feels uncomfortable accepting anyone's help and she will not, under any circumstances, let go of her little girl.

Earlier in the morning, the mom wearing the Broncos hat accidentally slid into Kamil, a 12-year-old boy who is here today to receive his chemotherapy all by himself. Though our wing of the hospital is quite warm, Kamil wears a huge black knit hat over his bald head and a bright yellow Nautica jacket throughout his entire visit. A black backpack is always draped over his shoulder but he never opens it, preferring instead to wander around the halls with his chemo bag, checking out his fellow patients and flirting with the nurses.

The nurses do their best to give Kamil a shred of the mothering that he doesn't receive at home. They talk to him and share their lunches with him and treat him like a boy that still has a full head of hair and doesn't have tubes sticking out of his arms. For the past two hours, Kamil has been on the phone every five minutes calling home to see if someone can come and pick him up. Each time, he lets the phone ring forever, hoping that someone will finally pick up after 14, 17 or 20 rings. Nobody answers his calls. When the tubes have been pulled from Molly's arms and it's time for us to head home, Kamil is still at the nurse's station, backpack over his shoulder, the phone cradled to his ear.

When we think of people who have a serious illness, we tend to think of the people that pop up on telethons, network news shows, and movies. These are the people who, more often than not, have a loving community of family and friends that surround them. People who will cry and talk with them until the wee hours of the morning. People who will bring over dinner after a particularly tough day at the hospital. People who will hold their hand and wipe away their tears when the end comes.

It's easy to think that everyone who deals with a serious illness has those people around them in their time of need. I used to think that way, but I'm smarter now.

Many of the folks who I see in my travels are very much alone. For every well-dressed couple that earnestly tells their story on the Variety Club Telethon, there's a sweet woman who fell madly in love with a good guy and had a baby, but when their baby was diagnosed with leukemia, the good guy turned into a weak guy who did a bad thing. For every kid who has a mom and dad who take off from work in order to hold their hand while they receive chemo, there is a kid who gets dropped off in the hospital parking ramp and picked up two hours late.

While I would never wish this experience on any parent, I cannot deny the blessings that Crohn's has brought to both our daughter and our family. Molly is a kid who is wise beyond her years. She's self-motivated, independent, and possesses a strong work ethic. All of those qualities are fairly unique in a 14-year-old and all of those unique qualities can be traced directly to dealing with Crohn's Disease. She can quietly laugh when one of her friends thinks the sky is falling because the supposed love of her life likes someone else. The transient nature of popularity and personal achievement are very clear to her. Massive amounts of homework, an obnoxious classmate, or a difficult teacher all take on newfound insignificance when compared to having a feeding tube inserted into your arm.

I hope I share that same sense of perspective. The value of family, friends, and work seems a lot more tangible now than five years ago.

It's just after 7:30 a.m. and I can hear the shower on in the upstairs bathroom. Tricia will be down soon to make chocolate chip pancakes for the kids and bring a jumbo-sized mug of tea with lemon out to me here on the porch. Zac will follow soon after to watch the baseball highlights on Sportscenter.

Always the last to awaken on Saturdays, Molly will stumble out onto the porch in a few hours to give me a kiss on the top of my head and wish me good morning. And as I wish my beautiful daughter good morning and think about the dark days in the past, I'll be thankful for this day together.

The Boy With One Name

A few weeks ago, I was loading equipment into my car after soccer practice when an angry mom approached me with what she felt was a serious complaint: "My son is not *Tommy* or *Tom,*" she hissed through gritted teeth. "His name is *Thomas.*"

I'm no Biblical scholar, but I'm pretty sure that this is one of the Seven Signs of the Apocalypse. Contrary to popular opinion, plague and famine won't signal the end of civilization. The onset of the End of Days will arrive when packs of Helicopter Moms flying precariously close to the ground demand that their sons be called by one and only one name.

The rational part of my brain understands that I'm overreacting. One controlling mom isn't the end of the world. Still, it feels like the end of something. Slowly but surely, it feels like adults are eliminating every fun part of being a kid.

At different times throughout my life, I have had a variety of nicknames. I've been called Hirsch, Timmy, Little Hirsch (the youngest of four boys in my family), T, Hacker, or simply Hack. I prefer some nicknames more than others. "Timmy" is like nails on a chalkboard to my ears, but I've always kind of liked "Hirsch."

Yet the truth is that one's own feelings about the nicknames we're given are never very important. One of my childhood friends could have called me Booger or Pinhead and I would have been happy. Because one of the sacred tenets of childhood is that when someone gives you a nickname, it means that you are part of the group. You are among friends. You belong.

One of the proudest moments of my childhood was the night my basketball coach started to call me Hacker. Tim was an insecure little punk who couldn't make a foul shot if his life depended on it. Hacker was a relentless defender that would happily run into a wall for a loose ball. Tim was a lazy student who spent a considerable amount of time wishing he were dating Cheryl Tiegs. Hacker was an important part of our team.

Young Thomas is an important part of our soccer team and his mom seems like a nice enough lady. There is a rumbling, hyper-caffeinated quality about her that I don't completely understand, but I think she clearly loves her son a lot. Still, I'm confused by her parenting decisions. What compels a woman to insert herself so deeply into the social interaction of her eight-year-old son? More importantly, how much friendship, laughter, and fun will her son be denied with his mother constantly hovering overhead and dictating that he can only be identified by one acceptable name?

I don't want to sound like the grizzled old coach who views parents as a necessary evil associated with coaching kids. For every obnoxious youth sports parent I've met over the years, I've met 50 fantastic parents—loving moms and dads who sacrifice a considerable amount of time and money to give their children a great life.

It's also worth noting that almost every parent I meet makes questionable decisions that I quietly pretend to ignore. If a parent insists on tying their nine-year-old's cleats for them, or zipping up their jackets "the right way," or cutting up their chicken for them at the dinner table, I think that's more than a little weird. I might wonder aloud to my wife how far Thomas's mom plans to take the one and only one name thing. Will she still be dictating the rules of identity to Thomas's teachers in high school or college? Perhaps I'll even express concerns about a generation of children whose creativity and independence is stunted by over-attentive parents.

But you'll never catch me sharing those opinions out loud in front of children. A huge part of my job as a coach is to support the parents of my players. If I walk past a 10-year-old kid who is rolling his eyes and wrestling away from his mom as she tries to zip up his coat, part of me wants to light a torch, paint my face blue, hop on a horse, and yell for the kid to break away from the oppressive force of his mother and follow me to freedom.

But I don't. Because it's my belief that if two authority figures challenge each other in front of a child, it compromises the respect that the kid has for all authority figures.

The situation with the Boy With One Name feels different. It seems clear that Thomas likes to be called Tommy, and that's the most important thing to me. Thanks but no thanks, Helicopter Mom, I'll call your son whatever I want.

Matt and Andy

In many ways, Matt and Andy were the same player. Both were 7-year-old boys that I coached in an U9 soccer league. Though they were very young, both boys had outstanding talent and raw speed. And as the third week of our season rolled around, both boys were suffering from a deadly soccer virus called Me-Ball-Net Syndrome.

Every talented young soccer player contracts the Me-Ball-Net virus at some point. They become so infatuated with their own skills that they ignore all external stimuli around them. Typical Me-Ball-Netters refuse to acknowledge their teammates and instead pretend that soccer is a game without positions, tactics, or teamwork. For them, soccer is a game of me, get ball, and go to net.

For a soccer coach, curing a child of Me-Ball-Net Syndrome can be a tricky thing. On one hand, we want players to have a burning desire to score as many goals as possible. On the other hand, it's important for young players to understand that soccer is a team sport. When players understand their responsibilities on the field, the team is more likely to score. When players ignore their responsibilities to the point that they shove a teammate aside so that they can assume control over the ball, it hurts the entire team.

By the fourth week of our league, I felt like it was time to lay the hammer down on Matt and Andy. For the previous three weeks, I had watched both boys continually embark on unsuccessful one-man voyages through six defenders to the opposing team's net. Patience and quiet instruction wasn't leading the boys to understand the value of teamwork. It was time to force the issue.

Before the game, I took both boys aside and told them that while I loved their energy and skills, I expected them to remember their roles on the field and play within their positions. "If I see you ignoring your position or taking the ball away from a teammate, I'll sit you for the rest of your shift," I said. "If you can't remember that you are part of a team, I'll replace you with someone who can." Both boys nodded their heads. Let's play soccer.

It's 10 minutes into the first half and Andy is playing forward. A teammate on the left side of field is dribbling up the sideline and looking to pass. I yell for Andy to go to the net and show himself as a passing target for his teammate, but old habits die hard. Instead of going to the net and showing for a pass, Andy runs toward his teammate, shoulders her off the ball, and starts making a run to the net.

To his credit, Andy immediately understood his mistake—I didn't have to say a word. He turned around and looked at me. I pointed to the sidelines and as he jogged off the field to sit out the rest of his shift, he mumbled a sincere apology.

"Onward, Andy," I replied. "Good for you for recognizing your mistake so quickly."

Ten minutes later, it's Matt's turn to completely ignore the concept of teamwork. He's playing defender and as he breaks out of his crease with the ball, he has four teammates who are showing strong targets for a pass upfield. Instead of passing to a teammate and holding his position, Matt ignores everyone and starts to dribble upfield. Who cares if there are six defenders between him and the net and who cares if the opposing net is at least 25 yards out of his position? Matt wants to score and he wants to score now.

I stop play and direct Matt to the sidelines. His reaction is the polar opposite of Andy's. Take a cup of slumping shoulders, add a few eye rolls, stir in some stomping and you've got one angry seven-year-old.

At halftime, Matt's father approaches me and he doesn't look happy. "Matthew says you won't let him score." I tell his dad that I want Matt to score a lot, but also that I want his son to understand how roles and responsibilities work on the field. More importantly,

I'm looking for Matt to see beyond his own self-interest and start working with his teammates.

This seems like a pretty simple and respectful response, so I'm surprised when Matt's dad says, "Fine, we're going home." My time as young Matthew's soccer coach was officially over.

After the game, Andy's mom approaches me and although she doesn't seem upset, I'm prepared for the worst. "I'm so glad you're Andrew's coach," she says. "Thank you for taking some extra time with him. He loves playing soccer, but we're still working on the teamwork thing." Given my encounter with Matt's dad at halftime, I wanted to jump in her arms and give her a hug.

Fast-forward 10 years. Matt and Andy both lived in my hometown, so I had the opportunity to watch both of them grow up over the years. As I write this, both are seniors in high school. Every time I see either boy, I'm reminded of that sunny Saturday morning just over a decade ago.

Both boys were outstanding athletes in elementary school. Matt excelled in travel soccer, hockey, and basketball. Andy was always the best player on the field in any sport he played.

In middle school, their paths started to steer in different directions. Andy continued to grow as a leader and an athlete. He played several junior varsity sports for his local high school while he was still in seventh grade. Matt quit playing team sports altogether. When I asked after him at local games, I was told that he had discipline issues in school that had led to a couple of suspensions. Outside of school, he started to play tennis at local tournaments, but my understanding was that he was more interested in throwing his racket and protesting line calls than developing his game.

In high school, Andy was the captain of the soccer, basketball, and track teams. Two weeks ago, he set a state record in the 100 meters and is generally recognized as one of the best athletes to ever come out of his school. Next year, he'll attend a Division I college on a full track scholarship.

The last time I saw Matt, he was leaning up against a fence and smoking a few blocks from his high school. The previous spring, he had been arrested for selling painkillers to some students at a local dance. My son says that he never sees Matt at school anymore. I hope he's OK.

When I think about Matt and Andy's stories, it is the contrasting perspectives on parenting that stand out to me.

Andy's mom viewed me as a partner while Matt's dad viewed me as an adversary.

Andy's mom trusted that she and I had similar goals: to help Andy and his teammates to become better soccer players and better people. Matt's dad believed that I was picking on his son.

Andy's mom created an environment to nurture her son's outstanding natural ability. Matt's dad created an environment that pampered his son and ultimately destroyed his ability to function as a member of a team.

Ten years ago, Andy's mom was focused on her son's personal development, and he ultimately turned into an all-star. Matt's dad wanted his seven-year-old son to be recognized as an all-star, and he ultimately grew to hate playing sports.

Future Ghosts and
Mr. Hair Gel

We are at a hockey game. It's a rare treat for him in a life consumed by graduate school, a part-time job, and starting a family of his own. This is a good idea. His wife is catching up on her sleep at home while my wife is excitedly baby-sitting our new grandson for the very first time.

It feels weird. We haven't been to a game in a long, long time. Yet some things never change. He still has every player's career statistics committed to memory. He still gets more excited when the mini-mites play between periods than when the pros are on the ice. And he is still the only human being I have ever met who loves those greasy three-month-old hot dogs they sell at the concession stands.

We order a beer and take our seats. He is tired and a little thinner than his mom and I would like to see him. Still, I'm not too worried. He's worked his way through difficult times before. The death of a good friend in high school and a challenging college internship in the inner city are just a couple of experiences that have helped him grow from a boy into a man.

If he wasn't a man three months ago, he is now. There's something about bringing a child into the world that will turn you into a grown-up real quick. Thirty years ago, the mystery and wonder found in a hospital delivery room radically changed my perspective on life, family and faith. It's clear that the birth of his little boy has had a similar effect on him. While my daughter-in-law is quick to note that it takes him at least 45 minutes to change a diaper, she is just as quick to privately—and lovingly—tell me how he loves to fall asleep with his little boy snuggled on his chest. We have been blessed with a fantastic daughter-in-law. She has married a very good man.

He suggests that we head home early from the game. Fatigue and an early day at work tomorrow are his excuse, but I think he just misses his family. As we head home after the second period, he gives me directions on the fastest route home and tells me that I'm nuts if I don't think the Sabres need a scoring defenseman to anchor the power play. Normally, I'd tell him he doesn't know what he's talking about, but tonight I don't care. We're listening to the third period on the radio and it's starting to snow and I'm spending some time with my buddy. I'm well aware that he's 30 years old now, but he's still my buddy. He always will be.

We pull into his driveway and quietly unlock the door to find his wife and baby sound asleep on the living room floor. We sit there and watch them for a few minutes; living, breathing light-and-beauty resting on a blanket in his family room. "What did you ever do to deserve all this?" I ask.

"What did you ever do to deserve Mom?" he laughs. "Or me?"

On any other day, I'd do my best to knock a straight line like that out of the park. Tonight, I just want to tell him the truth. "I don't know what I ever did to deserve your Mom," I confess. "Or you. You've grown into a good man, Zac, and you're a great dad, too."

My son isn't 30 years old yet. In fact, Zac is only 12. He is on the cusp of adolescence, that weird stage where girls are starting to look pretty and his parents are starting to look like morons. Suddenly, getting the right hair gel matters more than getting the right answers in school.

In my heart, I know that all boys go through this stage. Yet at least twice a day, I find myself fighting the urge to tie Mr. Hair Gel to the kitchen table and shave him bald. For now, the hair clippers stay in the bathroom cabinet upstairs and I'm content to daydream about a time and place when Mr. Hair Gel turns into Mr. Responsible Husband and Father.

Years ago, I used to dream about what it might be like to watch Zac pitch for the Yankees someday. Time passes quickly and as we both get closer to the time when my son will be an adult, my dreams have become less glamorous and more significant. I want my son to develop a strong work ethic. I want him to have the strength and courage to overcome adversity. Mostly, I daydream about a time when marriage and fatherhood will give Zac the same sort of daily miracles that he and his mom have given to me.

Mr. Hair Gel tests my patience now, but there will come a day when I'm sitting at a hockey game with a fine young man.

The Assassin

Part of my job involves supervising a group of a few dozen coaches who work almost exclusively with players age four to 12. Though we are an eclectic group of personalities, all of us enjoy working together. More importantly, we're all dedicated to doing great work with young athletes.

Around six to eight times a year, I receive a call from a mom or dad who is unhappy with the performance of one of our coaches. Half a dozen calls might seem like a lot to you but given the fact that our company teaches roughly 6,100 kids a year, I think that's a pretty good record. Heck, I've talked to elementary school principals who supervise schools of 600 kids and it's not uncommon for them get six complaints from parents before lunch on Monday.

I'd estimate that roughly 50 percent of the concerns that I've heard through the years are valid. Our coaches aren't perfect. Sometimes we make mistakes and every once in awhile, we make a huge mistake. More often than not, the mistakes relate back to me. On a few occasions, I've given coaches more responsibility than they were prepared to handle and every now and then, I've hired someone who just doesn't work out.

The remaining 50 percent are concerns that I find strangely fascinating. While some come from nice people who are just looking for a different type of sports program for their children, most come from parents who the folks in our office jokingly refer to as Character Assassins.

The last Assassin to contact our office was a very sweet mom who hated my guts. OK, maybe "hated my guts" is a little too strong. I don't think this mom hated me, she just thought I was a bad coach. In a conversation that she had with a colleague, the mom said that she wouldn't enroll her son in any league that included me as a coach.

I can't quote her verbatim because she never spoke directly to me, but as best I can tell, the root of her problem was that I was too tough on her son. She said that several times, I had embarrassed her son in front of the rest of the team and on two occasions, she had watched me reduce a child to tears. From her perspective, it didn't seem like I knew how to speak to children.

With the court's permission, I'd like to share my side of the story.

Her son was a talented six-year-old kid who I really enjoyed coaching save for one significant issue: he had very little self-control. Almost any time that he was placed in a small group, Aidan would pick, poke, push and/or grab the closest child to him. He wasn't a mean kid, but I don't think Aidan knew his own strength. More than a few of his teammates were intimidated by him.

A big part of the problem was that Aidan's mom gave us no support from the sidelines. In fact, it was clear that she found his behavior amusing. Her response to seeing Aidan commit felonious assault on another child was to giggle and shake her head, as if Aidan sticking his fingers up into another boy's nasal cavity was a cute thing that all boys do.

Three times during the season, I sat Aidan away from everyone else in the gym. Separating him away from the rest of the group was always used as a second or third resort—never a first—and I never sat him out without first giving him a clear warning. If that constitutes "embarrassing" a child, then I guess I'm guilty.

And for the record, I never made a child in Aidan's league cry. I'd guess that 90 percent of the kids in his league not only improved their soccer skills, but also had a lot of fun in the process.

In conclusion:

Aidan was a kindhearted little maniac.

Aidan's mom was clueless.

I'm perfect.

Just kidding. I make coaching mistakes every single night of every single season. Whether my mistakes are small or serious, I always try to acknowledge them, apologize, and learn.

In Aidan's case, my major mistake was failing to involve his mom in correcting his behavior. I assumed that she couldn't help me, that a lot of Aidan's misbehavior traced its way back to the way she indulged her son. That wasn't a fair assumption to make. At the very least, I should have given his mom a clear understanding of my concerns. Maybe hearing my concerns would have encouraged the mom to voice her own concerns about my abilities as a coach. Maybe we could have learned something by opening our ears and listening to each other. Maybe not.

Eventually, every parent will encounter a coach or teacher that is doing poor work. My experience is that many parents struggle to communicate their concerns to the coach. Some view coaches as crazed zealots who are obsessed with winning. Others assume that the coach is a thickheaded jock who can't understand words that have more than three syllables. The majority simply feel awkward about initiating any type of communication that is geared toward criticizing the coach's performance.

But what's the alternative? In Aidan's case, the failure of his mom and I to have a constructive discussion led me to lose a good kid from the league before I had helped him harness some measure of self-control over his actions. It led Aidan's mom to spread false rumors that I embarrassed kids and made them cry. Our actions were rooted in resentment based on assumptions about each other. Neither one of us made Aidan our highest priority.

As a coach who has had a lot of great (and some not-so-great) discussions with parents over the years, here are 10 suggestions to ensure that when you express a concern to a coach, your voice is truly heard:

- Register your concern immediately. It's tougher for a coach to fix a problem if you wait six weeks to address it.
- Like parents, coaches and teachers are authority figures. Never confront them or compromise their authority in front of your child.

- Look around. Do the rest of the parents in class seem as aggravated as you are? Are the other kids in class as unhappy as your child? Does the coach seem like a bad guy, an incompetent guy, or well-intentioned guy that is trying as hard as he can? Sometimes the problem is the coach, but sometimes the problem relates to you.

- Get a second opinion. Explain your concern to your spouse or a friend. Conclude your explanation with the following question: "Am I overreacting or do you think I should be upset about this?"

- Many of the concerns I hear about teachers and coaches are personality clashes. The coach isn't a bad coach and the parent isn't a bad parent, but together they have conflicting styles and philosophies. Is the object of your concern a bad coach or a good coach who does things differently than you would?

- Do not give a coach a free pass because he or she is a volunteer. Whether they receive a paycheck or not, every coach and teacher has an obligation to do great— or at the very least, competent—work with their players.

- Speak for yourself. Unless other parents have explicitly given you permission to speak for them, don't assume the role of parental spokesperson.

- Be completely honest. If you shade the truth, lie, or exaggerate, it only serves to compromise your credibility. On a related note, you gain credibility when you acknowledge your own mistakes. Assuming the posture that you're infallible and the object of your criticism has no redeeming characteristics whatsoever will rarely lead you to any genuine resolution.

- If you are able to reach some measure of understanding with the coach, don't hold their past transgressions against them. All of us are capable of making a mess of things, recognizing our mistakes, and growing from the experience.

- If the coach is rude to you or completely blows you off, talk to their boss. Everyone answers to someone.

The Summer Of Stunk

Shortly after our son saw the inside of the maternity ward at Sister's Hospital, he started kicking a soccer ball around. Zac has played a bunch of different sports competitively, but soccer has always been his first love. He has always been a pretty good player, and I have had a great time watching him play.

Actually, there was a brief period when Zac was 12-years-old when he wasn't a particularly good soccer player. My recollection of that period is that a freakish growth spurt robbed Zac of much of his coordination and speed.

My son's recollection of that period is more blunt: "I stunk."

Six years later, Zac and I can look back at the Summer Of Stunk and joke about it. Back then, it wasn't a laughing matter. Throughout most of his childhood, playing soccer was a source of pride and recognition for Zac. He was always one of the most talented kids on the field. I'm sure it boosted his young ego to hear other players and parents praise him. Slip me a teaspoon of truth serum and I'll admit that the praise boosted my ego, too.

Suddenly, there was no praise. Zac struggled to play a game that had always come easy to him. Almost overnight, he morphed from a mop-headed little bullet who could dribble circles around opponents into a gawky flamingo who regularly coughed up the ball up to the other team. Soccer was no longer a game that he equated with fun and accomplishment; it was an activity filled with failure and stress.

Inevitably, Zac's travel coach started to reduce his playing time. For the first time in his life, our son was sitting on the bench more than he was playing. It was a confusing and frustrating experience for him. I'd guess that dozens of questions floated around in his head. Questions like:

Should I be happy that some of my friends are playing more or angry that I'm playing less?

When my parents tell me that they are proud of me, do they really mean it or are they just being nice?

Aside from smoking cigarettes in an effort to stunt my growth and shrink back to my pre-growth-spurt size of six months ago, what can I do to play better?

To his credit, Zac never pointed fingers at anyone or blamed his coach. He recognized that the coach who was currently playing him one third of each game was the same guy who was playing him for the full game the previous year.

Tricia and I refrained from pointing fingers, too. As much as it broke our hearts to watch our son sit on the bench and stare blankly out onto the field, we recognized that his coach was the same guy we had always admired and respected. The rules and philosophy of the team hadn't changed. Zac had changed.

When our son began to spend more time on the bench, I kept my mouth shut. It was clear that he was frustrated and I didn't want to add any additional stress to the situation. The last thing he needed was a myopic, overzealous dad trying to be his therapist, best friend, agent, and advocate all rolled into one. If he wanted to talk about things, I trusted him to be the guy to initiate the discussion.

After a month or so, he did. When we talked, I didn't offer Zac any specific advice. After all, this was his problem to solve, not mine. Mostly, I just listened.

Though I didn't give him any advice, there were two points that I wanted to make during our conversation. First, I reminded Zac that I loved him and that I was very proud to be his father. I assumed that he already knew that, but in matters related to love and pride, it's best not to make assumptions with a 12-year-old.

Second, I suggested that Zac try to look at things from his coach's point of view. A coach looks for more than just talent from his players, I said. Given that his skills were faltering, I encouraged him to think about what else he could do to make his coach give him more playing time.

When Zac returned to practice a few days after our conversation, his coach approached me afterwards and asked me about Zac's change in attitude. He noted that Zac refused to be outworked by any of his teammates. Every drill, every wind sprint, and every minute of every scrimmage received his full effort. Years of relying solely on talent had led him to develop lazy practice habits. He obviously had decided that increased effort was the key to improving his skills and getting off the bench.

It wasn't easy. Early on, he mentioned that he had thrown up after a particularly tough running drill. Some of his teammates gave him a hard time for, in their words, "trying too hard." I didn't like the thought of Zac vomiting in the grass or dealing with peer pressure from his teammates, but I loved the idea that my son was willing to jump over some significant hurdles to meet a goal that was important to him.

Zac made another decision that was, in my opinion, pretty creative for a 12-year-old. At games, he refused to sit on the bench. When his coach subbed him off the field, Zac would grab some water and then stand and watch his teammates play. Without complaining, pouting, or saying a single word to his coach, he was sending a clear message: I have no interest in resting on the bench, but I'm very interested in playing on the field.

It didn't happen overnight—my recollection is that it took four to six weeks—but Zac returned to playing the full game again. He was a different player, more appreciative of the game and much more hard working. Being in the starting line-up mattered more to him when he had to work his butt off to get there.

As a parent, watching Zac play hard for a full game mattered much more than watching him score three effortless goals. Mostly, I was proud that he solved the problem with little guidance from us.

He didn't complain or wallow in self-pity. He didn't recruit his mommy and daddy to talk to the big, bad coach. At age 12, he had demonstrated more objectivity and maturity than most adults twice his age.

Zac is in college now and he still loves to play soccer. It's funny, but as I sit here writing this, I can't remember more than a few goals that Zac has scored in his lifetime. Ask me about wins, losses, and awards and I draw a blank.

But as long as I live, I'll never forget the sight of a 12-year-old boy on the cusp of becoming a young man. He is standing on the sidelines, yapping encouragement to his teammates, and respectfully refusing to sit on the bench.

Hooks

When I first started coaching, there was a growing sentiment that youth sports was heading toward extinction. Television was creeping from family rooms into the basements and bedrooms of American households. Atari, Pacman, and Donkey Kong were starting to consume the attention of American children. Back in the late 70s and early 80s, many of my fellow coaches and teachers were wondering if television and video games would eventually render youth sports obsolete.

Of course, it never happened. Playing ball with friends under sun and blue skies still exerts an enormous gravitational pull. Enrollment in youth sports leagues has exploded upward over the past three decades and there is no glimmer of extinction on the horizon. Video may have killed the radio star, but youth sports are alive and well and healthier than ever. That said, we are living in an age in which our children are being raised by appliances. The television, computer, cell phone, DVD player, iPod, and video game system all are used with ever-increasing frequency to occupy a child's attention while their parents are busy working, sleeping or playing.

One of the hidden attractions of all the technology that captivates our kids is that it comes equipped with features that allow a child to opt out of an activity at the first whiff of boredom. If they don't like what they find on a television channel or website, they can skip to the next selection. If a movie gets bogged down in too much dialogue, a mere touch of the fast-forward button allows children the opportunity to get to the good parts. If failure looms on the horizon of a video game, they can push re-start and start a game all over again.

All of these neat little features provide plenty of immediate gratification, but they tend to reduce a child's attention span to three milliseconds. In today's world of handheld gaming systems and fiber-optic network sprawl, it has never been more challenging to gain and retain the attention of a child. Here are a handful of things I try to remember when I speak to a group of kids:

Eye Contact- It sounds simple, but I have to battle a tendency to look past my players when I'm teaching to a full group. When I want to make an important point, it is much more effective to look my players directly in the eye.

Simple Words- Never use a 10-letter word when a five-letter word is available, and never assume a player under the age of eight understands a word with more than three syllables.

Expect a Verbal Response- I expect young athletes of all ages to speak to me in words. Grunts, shrugs, and eye rolls aren't examples of effective communication. Better to learn that at age seven than age 17.

Repetition of Key Phrases/Ideas- Ideally, coaches help create an inner dialogue for players, a voice players hear inside their heads while the game is running. I want that inner voice to be clear and concise. When executing a skill, the "inner voice" message that a coach gives to a player should rarely contain more than seven or eight words (ex. "attack space," "find your target," "switch fields.")

Mix It Up- Though I want everyone on the team to feel safe, I like my players to be on the edge of their seats, to never feel completely confident that they know what's coming next. I try to mix the tone, inflection, and volume of my voice. I frequently alter the posture of my students (standing, sitting, lying on back or stomach, etc.). Coaches who create the same teaching environment every day are begging for players to tune them out.

Silence- The empty spaces between words can be mesmerizing.

Hooks- A hook is a statement or action that precedes important information I want players to retain. For example, if I tell my players that I got hit by a train on my way to practice, but the night's lesson on passing is so important that I jumped out of the ambulance to make sure I made it to practice on time, the hit-by-a-train/jumping-out-of-the-ambulance part of the statement is the hook, and the lesson on passing is the important info. Common hooks that appeal to young athletes are humor, nonsense, violence, or any mention of the word "booger."

Teach From the Positive- I'm not one of those goofy guys who believes that a coach should always be smiling and making unicorn balloons for his players all of the time. Sometimes, kids need a coach to identify unpleasant truths or distribute a metaphorical kick in the butt. However, it is usually more useful to teach from a positive perspective. Telling a team, "I'd like to see everyone defend more like Rachel." is far more effective than saying, "We're defending like a bunch of wimps."

Humor- Children are far more likely to retain information if they are laughing when they receive the info for the first time.

Listen- When one of my players asks me a question, I often fall into the bad habit of formulating my response while he or she is still talking. Attentiveness is a two-way street. When my players have questions or thoughtful observations, I try to listen to them in the same way that I hope they listen to me.

Illustrate- When presenting new material to their players, many coaches rely on the old adage of "tell, show, and do." However, most of the coaches I've met over the years feel reasonably comfortable with telling their players what to do, but generally stink at demonstrating new skills and concepts. If a picture is worth a thousand words, a picture shown to a young athlete is worth 10,000 words.

Trust and Honesty- Children have finely tuned lie detectors implanted in the backs of their skulls. If they sense that a coach is full of crap or has ulterior motives, they will tune out in a heartbeat. Whether I'm delivering high praise or blunt criticism, I always want my players to be able to trust that I am telling them the truth.

The Food Chain

My work involves wearing many different hats. Teacher, writer and small-business owner are the biggest parts of my job, but there are lots of other things that I do each day. I like it that way. As someone who was born with the attention span of a flea, it's pretty cool to get up in the morning and know that I won't be doing the same thing all day long.

Still, it leaves me with an interesting dilemma. When people ask me what I do for a living, what do I tell them? For years, I picked out the most important part of my job and said, "I'm a teacher." But that response would usually lead to the following awkward exchange:

Nice Person at a Party: "Oh, you're a teacher? What grade?"

Me: "Actually, I work with kids of all different age groups. I teach kids to play sports."

Nice Person at a Party: "Oh, so you're a gym teacher? Where do you teach?"

Me: "All over the place. I'm actually not a gym teacher. My wife and I own a company that works with schools to coordinate instructional sports programs for kids between the ages of four and 12."

Which leads us to the awkward part of the conversation. At this point, people respond in one of three different ways, none of which is particularly flattering.

Sometimes, people smile and say *"So you teach kids to play sports for a living?"*

General Translation: "Seriously, what's your real job?"

The most insulting response is when a patronizing glaze creeps across someone's face and they'll say *"Oh, that sounds very exciting."*

General Translation: "You are the biggest loser I've met in my life and as much as I'd like to point my finger at you and start laughing hysterically, I'll pretend to be interested in your alleged "job" because I'm a nice person and I don't want to hurt your feelings."

The most frequent response is *"Oh, you own your own business?"*

General Translation: "Whew! For a second there, I thought you were a total loser. If you own your own business, I guess you must be a contributing member of society after all."

In the grand food chain of professional careers, anyone involved in teaching kids to play sports ranks somewhere between movie theater ushers and employees who use the phrase "Do you want fries with that?" as part of their job.

Think I've got an inferiority complex? Ask any individual who eats their lunch in a faculty lounge and they'll tell you that a basic caste system exists in every faculty lunchroom. The cool table usually consists of the hot shots from the English and arts departments and maybe a couple of the younger guidance counselors. Next on the status ladder are the suits from administration. Then comes anyone from the science or math departments who isn't wearing a pocket protector. Foreign language teachers and a few castoffs from the special education department are next in line. Gym teachers? They fall way down the ladder, just below the specialty teachers and one rung above the custodial staff.

Give any teacher two tablespoons of truth serum and they'll tell you what they really think of gym teachers: easiest job in the school... I wish I could hang out and play kickball with the kids all day... they don't even have to wear real clothes. The general perception out there from our peers is that physical education isn't real education. Anyone can do it.

The mindset that anybody can teach a child to hit, kick, catch, or throw a ball can have some serious ramifications. The most dangerous one is that we have little or no standards for the men and women who coach our children. If we believe that anyone can do the job, we'll accept anyone to do the job.

A few years ago, a friend of mine shared a quick bit of trivia with me: What do Mark David Chapman, John Hinckley, Ted Bundy, John Wayne Gacy and Jeffrey Dahmer have in common?

A) All rank among the most notorious criminals of the past 50 years.
B) All were the subject of bestselling books.
C) All volunteered their time as coaches in local youth sports leagues.
D) All of the above.

And the answer is... D!

While it's frightening to think that some of the most infamous murderers, rapists, and pedophiles all volunteered their time to teach America's youth to play sports, it's not surprising. It's rare that a youth sports organization interviews prospective volunteer coaches. Even more rare is an organization that trains its volunteers or evaluates the quality of their work. Low standards and a general lack of accountability have turned my chosen profession into flypaper for social misfits.

Think I'm exaggerating? Try a little experiment. Tomorrow, I want you to call up your local youth sports league and offer your services as a youth coach. If any of those organizations schedules you in for an actual interview, then I'll give you my car.

Just for fun, take it a step further. When you make the initial contact with the organization, act like a serial killer. During the course of the phone call, casually mention that you've got over 6,000 pictures of Jodie Foster glued to your bedroom wall. If that leads anyone to turn down your kind offer to coach, then I'll wash the car I just gave you every weekend for the next 10 years.

I'm happy to make either bet because it's a sure thing. See, I used to be the guy that answered the phone when you called to volunteer. Back then, we'd accept any warm body off the street that didn't carry a firearm and would promise to show up on time. It was a bonus if a coach didn't punch the referees or scream expletives at the kids. At one point early in my career, I was directed to accept non-violent criminals performing community service into the ranks of our volunteer coaches. *Good morning, kids. I'd like you to meet Mr. Twister. He got caught embezzling $40,000 from his church, but we think he'll make a really great basketball coach.*

Thankfully, some leagues have committed to conducting fingerprinting and background checks on all prospective coaches, but looking at the total picture, my sense is that the situation has only gotten worse. Ten years ago, we didn't read stories in the newspaper every other week about coaches assaulting players, referees knifing coaches, and parents brawling with each other. Our standards for youth coaches continue to hover between slim and none.

The Battle of Diminished Expectations

When my wife and I brought our first baby into the world, no one ever told us that we were signing up for a lifetime of battles. On that rainy spring night back in 1986, Molly Patricia Hirschbeck was a living, breathing miracle nestled warmly in our arms. Little did we know that she would also be a source of constant conflict in our lives.

The earliest battles that a new parent fights seem pretty small and silly. My wife and I can look back and laugh about the *Battle Of The Exploding Diaper* and the *Battle Of The Baby Who Won't Stop Crying.*

As a child grows older, so do the weight and significance of the conflicts. *The Battle Of The Kid Who Won't Do Her Homework* turns into the *Battle Of Why Can't I Wear Makeup* which inevitably leads to the *Battle Of Just Because Your Friend Does That Doesn't Mean That You Can, Too.*

For me, the biggest battle that we've fought with our kids has been the *Battle Of Diminished Expectations,* an epic struggle that usually follows the same basic script:

- *Kid gets an 86 on an important exam.*
- *Had Kid put forth a more responsible effort in studying for the exam, Kid could have easily earned a grade of 96.*
- *When Parent points out that Kid should have spent more time studying, Kid points out that Friend got a 72 on the exam.*

- *Parent notes that they aren't interested in Friend's grade. The issue is whether or not Kid studied as hard as Kid could for an important exam.*

- *Kid notes that not only did Friend get a 72 on the exam, but plenty of Other Kids failed the exam.*

- *Once again, Parent states that they have no interest in the grades of Friend or Other Kids.*

- *Kid notes that while plenty of Other Kids regularly engage in illegal and immoral recreational activities, Kid refrains from participation in those activities. Kid strenuously notes that Parent does not fully appreciate how lucky they are to have Kid in their life.*

- *For a third time, Parent notes that they have no interest in grades (or illicit behavior) of Friend or Other Kids. Their expectation is that Kid places a higher priority on studies and a lower priority on texting friends after school.*

- *Kid emphatically states that life would be far better if Kid lived with Other Parents and then stomps upstairs to bedroom to wallow in self-pity.*

- *Parent repeatedly bangs head against the kitchen wall to make the voices in head go away.*

Sex, substance abuse, and dirty diapers seem like small bumps in the road when compared to the diminished expectations that surround our children on a daily basis. There was a time not too long ago when we believed that anybody could grow up to be president of the United States, an astronaut, or the greatest quarterback in the history of the NFL. I'm not sure how or when or why it happened, but that unbridled optimism has withered away and been replaced by cynicism. Our kids are more likely to look at fallen pop stars and say "at least I'm not as messed up as her" than look at Nobel Prize winners and say "maybe I could be like him someday."

A huge part of the appeal of reality television is the opportunity for the viewer to feel superior to the lowest common denominator of human life. A teenager who is prone to wasting away hours of his life on texting and video games can take comfort in his ability to speak in full sentences and steer clear of sexually transmitted diseases, two traits that seem to evade the grasp of an average reality television star. Instead of reaching for the stars, they're content to feel superior to the mud.

Look, I'm not one of those helicopter parents who freaks out if their kid brings home an A- on a report card. I'm not on some secret mission to send my kids to Princeton or get them a scholarship to a Division I school. My daughter should have plenty of time to decompress and text her friends just as my son should have plenty of time to crash on the family room floor and play FIFA 2010 for a couple of hours. We all need to shut down and hang out the Do Not Disturb sign every once in awhile.

My frustration lies in the tools my kids use to measure effort and success. When they get an 85 on an exam, they inevitably search out the kids who got a 75 and think "at least I don't suck as bad as that kid." Just once, I'd like them to search out the kid who earned a 95 and model that student's effort and strategies.

In my book, an honest day's work isn't measured by looking at how you stack up against people who don't have a particularly strong work ethic. Rather, it comes from standing in front of a mirror and asking a simple question:

Did I do my best?

You Might Be A Helicopter Parent If...

You introduce your child to all the other kids at the playground and encourage them to play together.

Your primary motivations for volunteering at your child's preschool are to gain a behind the scenes look at how your child is handling the preschool curriculum, to identify potential friends that you'd like to invite over for play dates, and to make sure someone can open your child's juice box without making a mess.

When your child's swim instructor introduces herself to your daughter and asks your daughter for her name, you reply, "Her name is Alexa. Not Alex or Allie or Lexi. She prefers to be called Alexa."

When your child learned how to walk, he never fell down because you were always close enough to catch him.

When your toddler gets frustrated doing a puzzle, you find something else for him to do. Score double helicopter points if, while your child is engaged in the alternate activity, you finish the puzzle to make sure it's done right.

When your child colors, you always color with him to make sure he is staying within the lines.

Your child is eight years old and you still tie his shoes for him.

Your child is 10 years old and you still zip up her coat for her.

Your child is 12 years old and you still cut up his chicken up for him.

When your son falls down in soccer, his coach's first instinct is to tell him to get back up and reassure him that he'll be fine. Your first instinct is to tell him to stay down, assume that he is seriously hurt, and yell for somebody to call 911 while you check to see if his pupils are dilated.

At your first grader's open house, you automatically compare her Styrofoam egg carton sculpture to all the other kids' sculptures. Privately, you wonder who the hell Breanna Tomaselli is and how your child's classmate developed such a keen eye for structure and shape.

Your primary motivation in running the PTA book fair is the hope that you'll earn enough brownie points to be able to request that your child be placed with a good teacher next year.

You use the possessive pronoun when regaling disinterested relatives with tales of your child's athletic accomplishments, as in "*We* went all the way to the state baseball championships last year" or "*Our* team would have won if the ref had been able to see past his nose."

You sign your daughter up for ice skating lessons—not because she has expressed an interest in learning to ice skate, but because you always wanted to learn to ice skate when you were a little girl and never got a chance to try.

You finish your son's English paper for him because between basketball practice, student council, and community club, he can't do everything.

When your son brings home a B- on that same English paper, you call his teacher to inquire why it wasn't an A.

When your daughter locks herself out of her dorm room, her first call is to you instead of campus security.

When your child says, "I can't do this homework, it's too hard," your first reaction is that the work is too hard and teachers give out way too much homework today vs. when you went to school. It never occurs to you that your child is struggling to complete the homework because he is lazy.

When your child expresses the opinion that a teacher is a jerk, you decide that the teacher must be a jerk.

When your child complains that a travel soccer coach is an unfair, incompetent moron, you decide that the travel soccer coach is an unfair, incompetent moron.

When your child accuses you of being an overprotective control freak, you decide that she should see a therapist to work out some issues she has with authority figures.

You call potential employers for your child to see if they are hiring for the summer.

You videotape your daughter's basketball games in an effort to help her gain a better understanding of the Box and 1.

When Zac Kingston asks your daughter to the junior prom, you say "yes" before she does.

You privately wonder how much training you'd need to administer your child's immunizations all by yourself.

You have completed twice as many college applications for your child as you did for yourself.

You help your child cheat at the Annual Easter Egg Hunt: "Look to your left, Max. Lower. Now look to your right. Higher...higher... you're getting colder...now warmer, warmer...HOT!"

Your child is the only kid in kindergarten that has his own Blackberry.

When your son needs to take off from work to take the SATs, you call his boss to arrange coverage for him.

You consider yourself to be your child's best friend.

You are on a first-name basis with the director of housing at your child's college.

You often hear yourself using the phrases: "I don't mean to be a pain, but... ," "I know I sound like a helicopter parent, but I'm really not... ," and "My child would kill me if they knew I was calling you, but... ."

On your desk at work, there are eight photos of your children, one photo of your spouse, and no photos of your own parents.

Choosing Teams

I'm 46 years old and like most guys my age, I developed the ability to choose even teams by the time I entered the second grade. In the games I played with my buddies around the neighborhood, choosing teams usually went something like this:

1) *Two guys would volunteer to be captains.*
2) *One captain had the first pick.*
3) *The other captain chose the next two players.*
4) *Both captains would alternate choosing players until everyone was assigned to a team.*

More often than not, the teams we selected were evenly matched. On the rare occasion that one team dominated another, we'd stop the game and try to even things out. The solution to creating more balanced teams usually involved trading players, but sometimes we invented more creative solutions. My friend Mike was an All-Western New York baseball player in high school and around the time he turned eight, he became such a dominant hitter that we insisted he bat lefty to make things fair. I remember a few games in which Mike had to hit from his knees to keep the game even.

Whether we were playing street football in front of my house, basketball in my friend's backyard, or wiffleball over at the playground down the street, every kid in our neighborhood understood that creating balanced teams was an essential part of playing sports together.

When one team dominated another, the game wasn't fun anymore. Players grew angry and bored. Disagreements and bickering increased. Inevitably, guys would quit and go home. Once a few guys quit, the game was over, and once the game was over, the fun was over, too.

Like every other guy in America at the time, the guys in my neighborhood looked at sports differently than kids do now. Most of us were pretty competitive and we all liked to win, yet winning wasn't nearly as important to us as playing a long time. If we started a football game after dinner, it was far more important to keep playing until dark than it was to win the game. The key to playing for hours and hours was to create teams that were competitively balanced.

Things have changed drastically over the past few decades. With each passing year, it gets harder and harder to find a competitive game played between two evenly matched teams.

While out on my bike last summer, I came upon two youth sports-league games that left me shaking my head in disgust. One was a house-league soccer game and the other a Little League baseball game. The games were played less than a mile away from each other, and both games involved seven-, eight- and nine-year-olds.

The source of my disgust related to the competitive balance between the teams in each league. In the baseball game, it appeared as though the teams arrived to the field from two different solar systems. One team was comprised of big, strong nine-year-olds who had obviously played baseball since their pre-K graduation. The other team was considerably younger and smaller, only a few of the kids looked like they'd played baseball for longer than three weeks. Every single one of the kids on Team Goliath could hit and field like Ichiro Suzuki. The kids on Team Weakling tended to swing at the ball like a slightly-inebriated Kristi Yamaguchi.

When I left the game, the score was 26-0. It was the third inning.

The soccer game was worse. I arrived to the game shortly after the start of the second half and the score was 12-0. Again, it was experts vs. amateurs; a team of big, skilled players who had obviously played and practiced together for a long time "competing" against a group of younger kids who barely had any soccer experience. I stayed for most of the second half of the game and never saw the losing team advance the ball into their opponent's half of the field.

The difference in this game was emotion. The players and parents in the baseball game seemed resigned to the fact that they were going to get stomped on and merely wanted the innings to pass as quickly as possible, but at the soccer game, there was more than a little tension in the air. The goalie on the losing team was crying and a few of his teammates seemed on the verge of tears. A few of the parents on the losing team were clearly ticked off and began tossing not-so-subtle insults at the opposing team. Some parents on the winning team began lobbing insults of their own back at the losers. By the end of the game, a few parents were clinging to their lawn chairs with white knuckles and screaming at each other.

A friend of mine was one of the coaches of the dominant soccer team and when I spoke to him afterwards, he suggested that the occasional 22-0 blowout was "just part of the game." He even suggested that getting their collective butt handed to them in a sling by a superior squad was a good thing for the losing team, that the blowout would build the players character and make them try harder in the future. With all due respect to my friend, that's the biggest load of crap I've ever heard. A double-digit humiliation is exactly the type of thing that drives children away from sports. How much fun is it to be embarrassed in front of your parents? How much fun is it to watch your teammate start to cry after the 14th goal?

When a game ceases to be competitive, everyone loses. Coaches stop coaching. Referees alter their judgment in an effort to "even things out." Spectators lose interest or cringe in embarrassment. The losing team equates playing sports with injustice and humiliation. The winning team often mocks the game because they sense how shallow the victory actually is.

On the other hand, a contest between two evenly matched teams leads players to give a maximum effort. Learning and skill development is heightened for all players. The actions of coaches and referees are honest and true to the game. Spectators are focused on the contest and appreciative of the play of both teams. The losing team can find value in the loss and the winning team can take pride in the victory.

Almost every coach I've ever met will tell you that they'd like to play a complete schedule of games against evenly matched opponents. In their heart of hearts, I think most kids would prefer to lose an exciting game than yawn their way through a 22-0 victory. Which leads us to a slightly long but very simple question: if we can agree that competitive balance is essential to a healthy youth sports league, and if we can recognize that choosing even teams has always been an easy task for generations of eight-year-olds, then why is it so hard for the adults who manage youth sports leagues to make sure that every team in their league has a competitive chance to win every game?

It is my experience that the rampant competitive imbalance that exists in youth sports can be tied to three simple principles:

- Guys love to build stuff.
- Guys love to win.
- Few things give American men more pleasure than building something that wins.

For many youth coaches, the dream of building a championship team clouds our judgment. We're faced with a series of interesting internal dilemmas that see our "shoulds" face off against our "wants."

We know that all the teams in a league *should* be evenly balanced, but we really *want* to be a coach (or parent) on the team that's just a little better than everyone else.

We know that we *should* be teaching young athletes to value fair play and sportsmanship, but we also *want* our players to experience the joy of finishing in first place.

We know that we *should* openly question a coach who fields an all-star team in a recreational league, but we don't *want* to be perceived as the guy who complains after his team gets throttled.

All too often, our "wants" win out over the "shoulds" and our children suffer the consequences. At the introductory stage of a young athlete's development, we should be striving to help children equate playing sports with fun, friendship, and a sense of accomplishment.

In the era of 12-0 house league soccer, many young athletes equate playing sports with frustration, injustice, and failure. Some of the problems that plague youth sports leagues carry difficult and complex solutions. This problem, the lack of competitive balance in house and recreational leagues, is not one of them. The solutions are simple. Here is a basic framework for any prospective league organizer to help ensure that teams are balanced:

- The first day of the league is an evaluation day conducted by an independent group of three coaches. None of the evaluators should be the coach or parent of a child who participates in the league.
- Each child is given a grade based on experience and skill level. For example, the most talented players are graded 1, moderately experienced players are graded 2, and beginners are graded 3.
- An even amount of 1,2, and 3 players is assigned to each team.
- The following two restrictions are placed on player requests: 1) a coach may request that the coach's child and one additional player may play on the coach's team 2) parents in the league may request that their child play with one additional friend.
- If player-request chains of more than three players exist, they will be broken into smaller groupings.
- Children who don't attend the evaluation forfeit the right to make their own player requests or be included in another player's request.
- If obvious competitive imbalances exist, the league organizer reserves the right to make trades to correct those imbalances up to the third week of the season.

Though these guidelines are simple, they are not perfect. Even after taking these steps, coaches and parents will try to weasel together an all-star team of players. Parents of all-stars will deliberately sign up late for a league and request that their child play on the team of the parents' choice. They'll assemble a flow chart of 14 player requests designed to keep the strongest kids together. In recent years,

I've read accounts of parents who have threatened to sue a league in order to allow their children to play on the team of their choice. Parents and kids will go to ridiculous extremes to build and maintain a winning team.

League administrators should be ready for this fight and willing to take it on. How can we teach young athletes to compete if the games they play aren't truly competitive?

Psycho Stories

Place two people working similar jobs in the same room and within minutes, they'll start swapping what a friend of mine calls "psycho stories." Two grocery clerks will inevitably talk about the psycho-customer who, when stopped by security, claimed she didn't know how eight sirloin steaks found their way into her sweater. Sit two lawyers at the same table and one of them will tell a story about the psycho-client who wanted to sue Britney Spears in the hopes that it would help him to meet her. Nurses have lots of psycho stories, most of which involve bad tattoos, bedpans, or faulty hairpieces.

In my line of work, psycho stories usually involve a coach or a parent. Contrary to what you might think, it is the actions of adults—not children—that lead coaches to shake their heads and think, "You've got to be kidding me."

A story I often tell involves a Little League baseball game that I attended several years ago. I was at the game at the invitation of a couple of boys who had played for a soccer team I coached. Both boys must have been nine years old and playing for a team in the "AA" division which, as best I can remember, was open to eight- and nine-year-olds.

The game starts out and it looks like it's going to be a friendly affair. The umpire is a young guy, maybe 17 or 18, but he knows his stuff and takes the time to explain some of his calls to the younger players. The other team's coach is a little loud, but he's generally positive and encouraging to players on both teams. He becomes even more positive and encouraging when his team jumps out to an 8-0 lead in the first inning.

The score is 8-2 in the bottom of the third inning when one of my soccer players hits a double down the right field line with the bases loaded. Suddenly, it's 8-5 and things look and sound a little different on the other team's bench. The opposing coach is no longer clapping his hands and shouting "attaboy" every two minutes. Now he's pacing by the bench and shouting nonstop instructions to his bench. His calm, encouraging smile has been replaced by the grimace of a guy who looks like he just ate some really bad clams. One of the parents on our sideline notes that the coach must be stunned because his team hasn't lost a game in at least two years.

The next batter strikes out and the guy after him flies out to the second baseman. There are two outs and a runner on second when the catcher on our team steps up to the plate. He swings wildly at the first pitch and misses the ball by at least three feet. His next swing is even worse, so wild that it causes him to twist up like a pretzel, stumble a bit and fall flat on his back. As the pitcher delivers the third pitch, a couple of the kids on our team are picking up their gloves, certain that their teammate will strike out and end the inning. Five seconds later, those same players are throwing their gloves into the air and jumping up and down. Weird cosmic forces have somehow aligned to allow their catcher to mash a line shot to deep center field. Home run. It's 8-7.

It would be nice if my story had one of those tense bottom-of-the-ninth-two-outs-and- the-bases-loaded kind of endings. Sadly, it does not. After our catcher's home run, the floodgates opened and the kids on our side crushed every pitch that was remotely close to the strike zone. If memory serves me correctly, the final score was 18-12.

As the game went on, I remember being very impressed by the players on the other team. Most of those kids hadn't lost a baseball game in a couple of years, but there were no tears or tantrums from any of them. They held their heads high and played hard to the final out of the game.

Their coach? Well, let's just say that his behavior wasn't nearly as admirable. When it became clear that his team had no chance to win, his true colors started to show. His motto seemed to be "When the going gets tough, it's somebody else's fault." For a couple of innings, he yelled and screamed at his players—I have a vivid memory of him slamming his clipboard into the dirt and yelling, "Can't you guys do anything right?!!?"

Sometime around the bottom of the fourth inning, the coach directed his wrath at the umpire. There was a close call at second that went against his team, and it looked like he was going to pop a vein in his forehead. In the fifth inning, the coach started to violate one of the cardinal rules of the coach-umpire relationship: never argue balls and strikes with an umpire.

Some 17-year-olds would be intimidated by a 35-year-old guy taunting him. To his credit, this ump held his ground. He warned the coach once; he warned him twice; and when the coach still wouldn't shut up, he threw him out of the game.

Which leads me to the psycho-coach part of my story.

After embarrassing himself and his team, you might think that the coach would go home, hop in the pool, and cool off for awhile. If he had some class, maybe he'd even call the ump or the players on his team and apologize for his behavior.

Not this coach. After mocking the ump for a few minutes, he stomped off into the parking lot and stood there, arms crossed, glaring at the umpire. I watched him for a while and then, like most of the rest of the parents on our sideline, decided it was best to ignore him. The shortstop on the other team was making a fantastic diving catch on a pop fly when a mom on our sideline said, "What is he doing?"

By the time I looked over at the parking lot, the coach was driving away. Someone said it looked like he was doing something to one of the cars in the lot. A few of us walked over to take a look but we couldn't find anything that looked out of the ordinary. And then I saw it. The scene before my eyes was one of those things that are so strange that it took a few seconds to process what I was looking at. This coach, this 30-something adult, this supposed role model, *had ripped the windshield wipers off of the umpire's car.*

Twenty years later, I'm still shocked. What would possess a grown man to tear the windshield wipers off a 17-year-old kid's car?

I've often wondered if this guy's response to other types of adversity is similar in scope. If his boss reprimands him at the office, does he smash his windshield with a baseball bat? If his son doesn't eat all of his carrots at dinner, does he set his bike on fire?

Here's the scariest part of my story. About a month later, I'm out for a long run on a Saturday morning and guess who I see coaching the same team at a local baseball diamond? Jack the Wiper Ripper. It seemed pretty clear that he hadn't been fired or suspended. I'd bet a thousand bucks that he wasn't even reprimanded for his actions.

Perhaps the saddest part of my little psycho-story is that it's not an isolated incident. At a soccer tournament last year, I watched a bunch of parents openly taunt a group of 12-year-old Yemeni soccer players from Lackawanna. It was hard to tell whether their taunts were triggered by an inherent racial prejudice or the cooler of beer they had on the sidelines. Ask me sometime about the coach who had to be physically restrained after confronting me at a soccer game or the grandfather who punched a friend of mine after a baseball game played by six- and seven-year olds. Talk to any youth coach and you'll find that they all have psycho-stories of their own.

It always makes me feel good when a parent tells me that they think I'm a good coach, but sometimes I wonder if being a good youth coach is a lot like being the prettiest frog in the pond. Am I really a good coach or are the standards for my profession set so low that any guy who shows up on time and refrains from felony assault is considered to be above average?

If a grocery clerk or an auto mechanic vented their frustration by tearing off a customer's windshield wipers, they'd likely be fired. At the very least, they'd receive some sort of reprimand from their supervisor. If a Little League coach commits the same act, we roll our eyes and shrug our shoulders. It's almost as if we believe that dealing with nutjobs is a natural part of participating in youth sports.

Therein lies one of the great mysteries of organized youth sports leagues. Why do good people like you and me allow a small minority of morons to cast a shadow over the games that our children play?

The Pizza Mom

I was at Anderson's on Sheridan Drive a few nights ago, picking up some sandwiches and curly fries for dinner. When the summer nights get a little cooler, there is nothing better than an Anderson's roast beef sandwich to cut the chill in the air.

So there I was, dutifully standing at the counter and waiting for my order to be called, when out of the corner of my eye, I saw a family that used to be involved in the league that I run. There was mom (nice lady—kind of quirky), dad (a funny, talented guy—always liked him), big brother (shy, uncoordinated kid, must be 15 years old now, long since graduated out of our league), and little brother (11 years old, carbon copy of his older brother, played in our league up until last summer but now he's wearing another club's jersey).

It's clear that the mom and dad have noticed me, but they're doing anything they can to keep from catching my eye. It's like they're the pretty girl at the prom and I'm the geek that wants to dance with her. If they can pretend to be fascinated reading about all the different types of roast beef sandwiches that Anderson's serves, maybe the geek will just...go...away.

The thing that's causing mom and dad to stare intently at Anderson's menus has nothing to do with the geek at the roast beef window. The real source of their discomfort is the jersey that their youngest son is wearing. Instead of enrolling their son in the league that I run this summer, they have registered him in another league. This is an awkward moment.

Maybe it's awkward for them, but not for me. The way I see it, there are lots of good reasons why a parent might enroll their child in another league. Maybe younger brother wanted to play with his best friend or a cute girl from his neighborhood. Maybe he wanted to play for his school or his uncle is coaching a team. The league that I help to run isn't an organized crime family. There is no blood oath that's part of the registration process. If you want to dance with the guy with the long sideburns instead of me, it doesn't mean we can't still be friends.

I'm picking up my order and heading to the car when something funny happens. I hear a familiar voice say, "Hi, Coach!" It's the younger brother. He has noticed me and wants to come over and say hello. His older brother is trailing behind him. We catch up on where they're going to school and what they're doing for fun. It is nice to see that both boys are doing well.

The younger brother tells me he's playing in the ABC soccer league this summer. "Good for you," I tell him. "You having fun?"

"Yeah, it's fun. But it's not the same." He says, "I scored five goals this year."

"That's great!" I say as I punch him in the shoulder. "You should be proud."

Out of the corner of my eye, I can see mom and dad reluctantly moving over to join the conversation. They pretend that they didn't see me because they were engrossed in reading sandwich menus, and I pretend that I didn't see them pretending to be engrossed in reading sandwich menus. Weird.

We finish up our conversation and as we're about to part ways, the mom leans over to me and whispers, "He really wanted to play in your league this summer, but the ABC league is $10 less and the kids get a pizza party at the end of the season."

Huh? My brain is stuck. I can't process what the mom is trying to tell me. It's like she is saying, "He really wanted to play in your league this summer, but blue mountain lion drives peanut butter standard transmission in the Ghana." My head is spinning. All I can think of to say is, "Well, good luck."

This summer, parents have been especially kind in telling me how much they appreciate the coaches in our league. By my count, I've received eight e-mails, half a dozen calls, and heard from at least a dozen parents who have approached me at the field to say nice things about the men and women who coach in our league. Any time a parent takes time out of their day to pay us a compliment, it means a lot.

So what does it say about my twisted personality that I can't stop thinking about the Pizza Mom? At the risk of sounding arrogant, we did fantastic work with both of her boys —and I'm not just talking about soccer skills. We brought both boys out of their shell, built up their self-confidence, and helped them to communicate and cooperate with their peers. Neither boy is a great athlete, but both of them love to play soccer.

This might sound childish, but we have a seven- to eight-year history with those two boys and it bugs me that their mom is willing to toss that aside for 10 bucks and a few slices of pizza.

These are the things in my life that drive me crazy. There are parents walking on this planet who don't care if I'm a good coach or a bad coach. They don't care if I ever learn their son's name or conduct practice sessions that are fun and challenging for every member of the team. In evaluating the potential benefits of a youth sports league, they look for the pizza. Pepperoni, cheese, and 10 bucks are what differentiate good youth sports programs from bad.

My wife thinks I have a compulsive need to be loved by everybody. I think I have a compulsive need to raise the standards we use to separate good youth sports leagues from bad. Who is right? Probably both of us.

The T-Ball Calls

Spring is just around the corner and it won't be long before the days grow longer, the tulips bloom and the temperatures spike up over 60 degrees. For most Buffalonians, the arrival of spring is something to celebrate. For me, spring means that I'll soon have to deal with four words that strike fear into my heart.

The T-Ball Phone Calls.

I get at least 30 of them these days—more and more come in every year. Though the calls come from all over Western New York, all of them follow the same basic script:

Eager T-Ball Parent: *"Hi, I'm interested in registering my son for your T-Ball program..."*

Me: *"Great, we'll be happy to have you with us. How old is your child?"*

Eager T-Ball Parent: *"He's four."* (The more devious parents will say something like, *"He's almost five"* or *"He'll be five in six and a half months."*)

Me: *"Oh, I'm sorry. Our program is for five- and six-year-olds. The earliest that your son could play with us would be next summer."*

Eager T-Ball Parent: *"Really? (cue the violin). He's going to be so disappointed! Baseball is his favorite sport! When he comes home from pre-K, he spends hours out in the backyard throwing the ball up into the air and catching it. Did you know that his first words were Mama, Dada, and Derek Jeter?"*

Me: *"Is that right?"*

Eager T-Ball Parent: *"Oh, yes! (Cue an entire orchestra of violins.) He's got two older brothers who play Little League and he can't play. I feel*

151

so sorry for the little guy. During games, he just stands behind the backstop with his little nose pressed up against the fence. When I was tucking him into bed last night, he looked up at me and said, 'Daddy, why can't I play baseball?' "

Me: *"I'm sorry, but I can't make exceptions. It has nothing to do with your son. These days, it's a question of liability insurance. If a parent filed a claim against our program and we were found to have knowingly hosted underage children in the class, it could bankrupt us."*`

Eager T-Ball Parent: *"But you let four-year-olds in your soccer program!"*

Me: *"Yes, we do."*

I should stop here to mention that if Eager T-Ball Parent knows that we have soccer programs for four-year-olds, he also knows that the age restriction for T-Ball is five and six. This isn't a blind call from a new parent, this is a call from a parent who is familiar with our program and is calling to try and weasel his son into class.)

Eager T-Ball Parent: "That's not fair. If you let four-year-olds play soccer, you should let them play T-Ball."

Me: *"Actually, they're two completely different sports. Soccer is a fast-moving game with simple rules. It's easy to understand and easy to play. Baseball is much more abstract. The rules of the game are not only complicated, but subject to change based on a variety of different factors. More importantly, the skills involved in baseball are much more difficult to execute. Just the simple act of throwing a ball requires a series of complex muscle movements—each one dependent on the other."*

Eager T-Ball Parent: *"Well, you've never seen my son. (Cue the music from the climactic scene from* The Natural *where Roy Hobbs smashes a home run into the lights). This kid can catch everything that I throw to him. Grounders, pop flies, line drives—EVERYTHING! He was able to hit a pitched ball when he was still in Pampers. The other day, a friend of mine from the sheriff's department was over at the house and he clocked the boy throwing a 71 mph fastball on his radar gun! And you're telling me that this kid isn't ready to join your crummy T-Ball program?"*

Let me stop here a second time to point out two important things: First, only 10 percent of anything that this dad has said to me is true. While his son might have above-average gross motor skills, you can bet that he catches only 25 percent of the balls thrown to him and that he still twirls around like Kristi Yamaguchi every time he swings a bat. Parents are never models of objectivity—especially Eager T-Ball Parent. Second, note that in a matter of 30 seconds, Eager T-Ball has gone from desperately wanting to register for our program to insulting it. For some, this might seem like a weird transition, but as someone who has had this conversation 420,000 times, I can tell you that it's normal. It's always easier for Eager T-Ball Parent to call our program names than it is to look in the mirror and admit that there's something kind of strange about wanting your four-year-old son—a boy so young that he still enjoys the taste of his own boogers—to play organized baseball so badly that you'll antagonize a coach to get him enrolled.

The conversation lasts another minute or two. I remind Eager T-Ball Parent that it's nothing personal against him or his son and he tells me I'm being unfair a few more times. By the end of the call, neither of us is feeling real good about ourselves. Eager T-Ball Parent is upset because he'll likely have to spend another year playing catch with his son out in the backyard. I'm frustrated because in our current culture, more and more parents feel compelled to stuff their child into a structured instructional sports program as soon as humanly possible.

It's hard to understand why Eager T-Ball Parent ignores the value of an unstructured sports program. Instead of stressing out about age restrictions and worrying about getting a jump start on college scholarship money, why can't he just take his four-year-old boy to the park with some of his friends and throw the ball around?

As recently as the early 1970s, children were allowed to slowly awaken from a post-amniotic fluid haze around age three. It wasn't until puberty kicked in around age 13 that their parents would expect them to occasionally behave like an adult. Back then, the duration of a childhood was roughly 10 years. Today, a kid is lucky to have five good years to goof off, stir up some trouble, and just be a kid.

Parents of my mother's era seemed intent on making sure that their sons and daughters had a childhood that was not only healthy but long lasting as well. How many times did an adult in your family wag their finger at you and say, "You're growing up too fast"?

In the eyes of my generation of parents, a child can't grow up too soon. Whether we're dragging our three-year-olds to have their ears pierced at the mall, organizing elaborate preschool graduation ceremonies for our four-year-olds, or coordinating a Valentines Day dance for our 10-year-olds, today's parent believes that a child must always take the shortcut on the road to becoming a grown-up.

Youth sports are an extension of that warped mentality. When I first began teaching kids to play sports, the average age at which a child was allowed to play in competitive leagues was age eight or nine. The prevailing wisdom at the time was that it was unhealthy to throw a kid who was barely out of kindergarten into an environment filled with technical and tactical instruction, winning and losing, and scoreboards and standings. Adults believed that if you stuffed too much onto children's emotional plates, it would overwhelm them.

Today's young athletes are forced to handle the highs and lows of competitive sports by the time they reach the first grade—whether they like it or not. By the time they are eight years old, most young athletes have been exposed to all of the accoutrements of competitive sports (uniforms, trophies, playoffs, etc.) for a couple of years. With 10 years of competition under their belts, it should come as no surprise that a high percentage of kids burn out and quit playing sports altogether by the time they enter middle school.

A child will only be four years old for 365 days and then it's over. They'll never have another chance to be four again. Some parents spend that year enjoying the blessings and challenges of raising a four-year-old child while others spend each of those 365 days wishing that their four-year-old was actually a six-year-old. Which group of parents has a better chance of raising a happy, responsible and stable child?

Even a four-year-old knows the answer to that question.

Everybody Makes The Team

For years, I have volunteered to coach a travel soccer team for a local club in my community. One of the best parts of my job is speaking to parents whose child has made the team for the first time. Our club runs a very strong travel program and many players and parents can barely contain their enthusiasm when I invite them to join us.

Of course, the worst part of the job is telling parents that I don't think their child is ready to play on a travel team. Surprisingly, most moms and dads are very understanding. Most of the parents I speak to basically say something like "yeah, we really weren't sure that he was ready, but we thought we'd give it a shot."

Last week, I talked with a mom who attended travel soccer tryouts at another local club in the area. After 30 minutes, she and her 10-year-old son left early. "There was really no tryout," she said. "They accept everybody who signs up and tell you that they will find a team for you. They have no clue who is going to be coaching these teams. They were searching for coaches at the tryouts." Maybe this mom is exaggerating or perhaps she misunderstood the whole tryout procedure, but I tend to believe she is telling the truth. I've been hearing similar stories about the club for years.

The club's website seems to confirm the mom's story. They point with pride to the fact that "We had a 99% placement ratio last year!" It sounds nice, but is that really a good thing? It stretches the boundaries of reason to suggest that out of all the kids that tried out for the club's travel teams last year, only one percent were deemed not ready to play travel soccer. Something is wrong with this picture.

The picture becomes a little more clear when, in another part of the club's website, it notes that there are enough players to field seven U10 travel teams—three more than the previous year. My guess is that the 99 percent placement ratio and three new U10 teams have little to do with placing young soccer players in a program that is appropriate for them, and everything to do with making the club bigger!! And bigger!!! And bigger!!!!

Of course, the club will never admit to its ambitions. I'm guessing that its explanation for the 99 percent placement ratio is that it wants to make travel soccer inclusive to all players. They'll put an arm around your shoulder and tell you not to listen to guys like me. They'll call me an elitist and a snob, and they'll tell you that if your child wants to play travel soccer, then who are we to stand in your way?

The way I see it, it's my job to stand in your way. If I steer your child into a travel program before they are ready, they'll be playing among bigger, stronger, and more talented kids. Most of the fun associated with playing soccer will evaporate when your sons or daughters are losing all of their games by lopsided margins and getting their butt kicked all over the field.

A clever trick that some clubs play to deal with the butt-kicking issue is to assemble a group of pseudo-U10 players and register the team in the lowest level of travel soccer imaginable. If the pseudo-team is registered in the FFF Division (as opposed to the A or B Division), at least they'll win a few games and everyone will walk home happy.

This trick is inherently dishonest in that it misleads players and parents into thinking that they are playing legitimate travel soccer. Playing in the FFF Division of a U10 travel soccer league is akin to enrolling a high school student in an AP English class where the assigned reading includes *The Sneetches* and *Harold and the Purple Crayon*. A student can sit in a class called AP English and her parents can proudly tell the neighbors that their kid is taking AP English, but if the curriculum for the course contains Dr. Seuss and finger-painting, it ain't AP English.

Sadly, that clever little trick only postpones the butt-kicking for most players. Sooner or later, usually in U11 or U12, all the members of the FFF Division team are going to be forced to play genuine travel soccer and when they do, they are in for a rude awakening.

Thirty years of coaching experience tells me that pushing a kid prematurely on to a travel team drastically increases the chances that they'll quit playing soccer in a year or two. A variety of national studies tell us that 60 to 70 percent of young athletes quit playing team sports by the time they reach age 11.

I don't want your child to quit in a year. I want them to grow to love playing team sports and appreciate the value staying healthy and fit. Better an inexperienced nine-year-old has fun in a recreational soccer league than feels overwhelmed in travel soccer.

My guess is that the club with 99 percent placement doesn't share my goals. They want your travel soccer registration fee and they want it now. If your child has a miserable experience playing for an inexperienced coach and quits after a year, that's the cost of doing business.

Young athletes deserve more than that. They deserve league administrators who recognize young players as people, not profit. They deserve ethical coaches and administrators who protect the best long-term interests of their players.

Participation Trophies

When my son was five or six, a steady stream of awards and trophies began to flow into our house. Zac's pre-K diploma was followed by a soccer trophy, which was followed by a kindergarten graduation certificate, which was followed by a T-ball medal, which was followed by a ribbon for participating in a fire safety coloring contest. Shortly after he completed the first grade, I put up three big shelves in his bedroom to hold all of the awards he had received during the first six years of his life and for all of the trophies, plaques, medals, ribbons and certificates that I expected he'd bring home in the future.

I remember that Zac was excited when I put up those shelves. He seemed proud to arrange the trophies so that they'd catch the eye of anyone who entered his room. But by the time he completed third grade, most of the pride and excitement associated with receiving a trophy was replaced with indifference. At the end of every tournament or season, we'd go through the same basic ritual: Zac would respectfully shake the hand of the teacher or coach who gave him the award, toss the trophy in the back seat when we returned to our car, and then I'd fish the trophy out of the car a few days later and place it on one of the shelves in his room.

When I looked at my son's teammates, it became clear that Zac's perspective on trophies wasn't particularly unique. As they picked up their award, every player dutifully shook their coach's hand and none showed any real emotion. The fact that the awards didn't mean more to Zac or his teammates struck me as rude and ungrateful. His coaches and teachers were devoting their time and money to recognizing my son's accomplishments. Why did the assortment of plastic, metal, fabric, and wood sitting on those three shelves matter more to me than it did to him?

I finally solved the trophy puzzle when Zac was 15 years old. His soccer team had played very well in a tournament filled with strong competition. At the conclusion of the tournament, Zac's coaches and captains recognized him as the team's MVP of the tournament and gave him the trophy the team had won for finishing first in its age group. That trophy stayed in the front seat on the car ride home. Not only was it carried into our home and immediately shown to his mom and his sister, but it was allowed to be placed on our mantel for a few weeks so that some of his family and friends would see it.

The thing that separated that trophy from all the others was that he truly earned it. Fathers are never truly objective in evaluating their son's athletic accomplishments, but trust me when I tell you that Zac played outstanding soccer that weekend. In a tournament filled with talented players, he was consistently one of the strongest players on the field. The fact that he was the only player in his age division in the entire tournament to receive that trophy was not lost on him. For the first time in 15 years, he felt honored to receive an award.

All of the other sports trophies that he had accepted over the years were the same trophies that were given out to all the other kids. For Zac, the obligatory trophy at the end of the season was a part of playing sports, sort of like a jersey or a pair of socks. Looking back, it was foolish of me to expect my son or his teammates to show genuine gratitude at receiving a piece of plastic and marble that had no real emotion or meaning attached to it.

The current system that most leagues use in handing out awards to players seems filled with waste and unhealthy messages. Assuming the vast majority of players are like my son and leave most of their trophies in the backseat of the car, why are youth sports leagues spending tens of millions of dollars on trophies that instantly turn into dust collectors? For the minority of kids who are truly invested in receiving a participation trophy at the end of every season, is it a good idea to hand out awards to young athletes just for just showing up and doing what they're supposed to do?

Forget about health care reform and tort reform; what the United States really needs is trophy reform. Unfortunately, changing the way that we give young athletes awards is only slightly easier than reforming health care. Suggesting that it might be a good idea to give fewer trophies to kids is akin to suggesting that it might be a good idea to punch them in the face if they don't show up on time for the game. No one wants to be the guy that suggests we should do less for our kids.

What the heck, I'll be that guy. Here are a bunch of suggested reforms for trophies and award ceremonies in youth sports. If you take one of these to the board of directors of your local youth sports league and they call you a coldhearted barbarian, wave this page over your head and blame me.

Our first reform dictates that no trophy or award shall be given to any child under the age of six.

Sounds like we're snatching candy out of the hands of babies, doesn't it? In fact, what we're trying to do is keep kids from growing up too fast. Prohibiting children from receiving awards during their first five years on the planet increases the likelihood that a trophy given to them at the ripe old age of eight or nine will be more meaningful.

If anyone suggests that the denial of plastic and metal sports figurines attached to marble bases is cruel and unusual punishment for a preschooler, ask them this question: What exactly are the criteria for handing a trophy to a four-year-old?

"Congratulations, Max, you usually kicked the ball in the right direction."

"Good job, Maggie, you never came close to scoring this season but you always wore your jersey."

"No one raised a hand and politely asked to go to the bathroom quite like you did this year, Thomas, and it gives me great pride to award you the Southside Soccer Association Phillip Gloudette Medal of Freedom."

If we're completely honest with ourselves, the primary purpose of playing Pomp and Circumstance as a line of four-years-olds gathers to receive their Lil' Dribblers soccer diplomas is to give marginally unstable moms and dads an opportunity to applaud, cry, and take photographs. The four-year-olds who actually receive those diplomas will forget the experience by the time they eat their Cocoa Puffs the following morning.

Reform #2 says that participation trophies will be given out to players between the ages of six and eight.

Go ahead and call me a hypocrite for railing against the evils of participation trophies and then advocating that we hand them out to children for three years. All I'm suggesting here is that we spread a little love to the beginner. Traditionally, six to eight is the age at which most young athletes begin to play on a team, wear a uniform, and play games against other teams. Giving every child an athletic award at the conclusion of each season seems like nice way to reward young athletes during their formative years. Also, it insures that every kid who plays sports by the age of eight will have at least one trophy collecting dust in their bedroom.

Reform #3 dictates that from age 9 to 10, small participation trophies will be given to all players in conjunction with up to five larger individual awards.

We'll call these the transitional years, a period of 24 months when we acclimate kids to the idea that awards are given for actual achievement. By now, kids have learned that everyone doesn't always get the same test grade in school and only one person can have the last piece of pizza at dinner. It shouldn't be too difficult for a nine- to 10-year-old to understand that some players receive small trophies and some receive big ones.

The big trophies should be restricted to the following five categories: Offensive MVP, Defensive MVP, Most Improved Player (MIP), Sportsmanship Award, and a Coaches Award (which allows the coach to recognize a player for anything that stands out to them). Because three out of five big trophies are based on effort and character more than individual talent, every member of the team has a legitimate shot at winning one of the big awards.

Reform #4 says that participation trophies will not be distributed once a child turns age 11, and no more than five trophies for individual achievement will be awarded at the end of a season.

By the time a young athlete enters middle school, they play sports to have fun, to be with their friends, to win, to get better, or to represent their school or community. Only a tiny fraction of middle school and high-school kids play sports to receive a plaque or trophy at the end of the season.

Our fifth reform simply encourages coaches and parents to find alternatives to traditional trophies, plaques, and medals.

One of the best high school coaches I've ever met keeps a journal of every game his team plays throughout the season and at the team's awards banquet, he gives a copy of the journal to every member of the team. At the conclusion of the banquet, his players can always be found poring through the coach's journal while ignoring a two-foot trophy resting on the table in front of them.

A dad on my son's high-school soccer team took dozens of photos at every game. At the end of the season, each player was presented with a CD filled with photos of every member of the team in action. My son will always treasure those photos.

A friend of mine who coaches a girl's high-school basketball team diverts all the money budgeted for trophies toward a family party at the end of the season. The main event of the party is a parent-player basketball game that is recorded and shared on a DVD sent to all players a few weeks after the party.

My own alternative to trophies is to write a handwritten note to every one of my players at the end of the season. I don't want a season to conclude without every one of my players understanding how much I appreciate their unique contributions to the team.

An award or trophy has genuine value if it stands the test of time. Most of us box up our trophies and plaques and carry them up to the attic shortly after we graduate from high school. A coach's journal, a handwritten note, a CD filled with photos, or a DVD of a parent-child game have a greater chance of turning into keepsakes we carry with us for the rest of our lives.

The sixth and final reform requires that every coach, parent, or administrator charged with ordering trophies for their league ask the following three questions before placing their order:

Are these awards showering players with empty praise or are they recognizing players for genuine achievement?

A year from now, will these awards mean something to the majority of recipients or will they be buried under a pile of laundry?

Can I use the money budgeted for trophies on something else that might have a more tangible positive impact on our players?

Flea Flicker

For years, I have danced around the edges of moving somewhere else and starting over. Part of my restlessness relates to the temporary fits of insanity associated with being male and 45 years old, but there are other more grounded reasons for moving away. The oppressive tax structure and inbred political corruption in New York State often feels like a 40-pound weight on my shoulders, and the older I get, the more I bristle at the thought of plowing, shoveling, and tunneling through another Buffalo winter.

Three things keep me rooted in Western New York: my wife, September, and October. My wife has no interest in moving somewhere else and since I'm very fond of waking up next to her every morning, moving to parts unknown is currently not an option. September and October? They are the most beautiful 61-day span in my hometown.

Shortly after Labor Day, Buffalo becomes a magical place to live. The air is cleaner and the nights are cooler. Yellow school buses filter back into our neighborhoods and with them comes the laughter of children. I often find myself tripping over things because the fall sky is such a remarkable sight: enormous gray-white clouds cutting across a brilliant blue sky, oak and maple leaves burning brilliant reds and oranges, Canadian geese honking in formation to warmer climates, a giant harvest moon hanging low on the horizon.

Along with fall comes the greatest game ever played. We play it in backyards and parking lots, open fields and 70,000-seat stadiums. We play it with two and 22 players, wearing an old high school t-shirt and wearing 30 pounds of equipment, with our friends and against our sworn enemies. Football is an essential part of a fall weekend in Western New York.

For the past 15 years, I have been involved in running flag football leagues that annually serve several hundred kids between the ages of seven and 12. For the older kids in these leagues, my primary role as a coach is to call plays in the huddle and get out of the way. For younger age groups, coaches serve as quarterbacks for a variety of reasons. Young players tend to throw repeatedly to the best player on the field; a coach can distribute the ball around to more players. An average seven- to nine-year-old's arm isn't developed to the point where he can consistently throw deep; a coach can throw a deep pass more accurately.

There is one more important reason why our coaches step in to quarterback teams of younger kids and it has nothing to do with helping children. Most members of our coaching staff are older guys who love football, miss playing it every day, and jump at the opportunity to step in and be QB1 again. Who cares if our teammates weigh 60 pounds and still trick-or-treat on Halloween? When a man of any age flings a football as far as he can and it is caught by a teammate, we are transported back to the time when we learned to throw a perfect spiral from our big brother, or proved our toughness by quickly getting up after a vicious tackle, or gasped for air at the bottom of a pile of our friends. At least in part, we love football because it connects us to the best parts of our childhood.

When I am quarterbacking a team of young football players, the part of football that I love most is the Flea Flicker. It is the most deadly trick play in the flag football playbook. There are variations, but a basic Flea Flicker works like this:

- *the quarterback hands off the ball to the running back;*
- *the running back cleverly fakes a running play by sprinting two or three steps forward;*
- *sensing a running play, the opposing defenders leave the man they're guarding and sprint toward the running back to pull his flags;*

- *at the last second, the running back pitches the ball back to the quarterback as a collective rumbling of awe and excitement starts to gurgle from the crowd on the sidelines;*
- *the quarterback passes the ball deep to a receiver who is sprinting down the sidelines;*
- *time stops for a moment as the lone receiver adjusts his speed and body position to catch the ball, the quarterback jumps up and down at the approach of an imminent touchdown, and the crowd on the sidelines makes a noise that sounds something like "whuuuuuuuaaaahhhhh";*
- *the receiver catches the pass and gallops into the end zone as the crowd goes wild.*

Everyone who loves football loves the trick play. While we all recognize that the four-yard run over the right tackle and the six-yard slant are essential parts of football, it is the trick play that captures our attention and imagination. When we purchase a ticket to an NFL or college football game, some of us are purchasing the right to drink mass quantities of cheap beer in the parking lot and pass out on the hood of our cars. Some of us are purchasing the right to paint our entire bodies blue and dance on our seats every time our team scores. Yet I think that when most of us pass through the turnstiles, we are purchasing hope. Hope that at any time when we least expect it, we'll see something we have never seen before and may never see again. Let little boy blue and the unconscious guy in the parking lot chirp about the virtues of the four-yard run and the six-yard slant; I want a trick play.

Give me the Reverse, the Double Reverse, or better yet, the Fake Double Reverse. I'll pay double the price of admission to see the Statue of Liberty, the Halfback Option and the Hook and Ladder all in one game. Only wimps willingly give the ball to the other team; be a man and call a Fake Punt or an Onside Kick. Just once, I'd like to sit in a stadium and see grown men in helmets execute the Fumblerooski to perfection.

OK, maybe I'm going a little overboard. Trick plays may make the crowd go wild, but they also come with great risk. With the stakes in college and pro games so astronomically high, it's easy to understand why coaches at those levels don't use them more frequently. One failed Fumblerooski can cost a team millions and lead a coach to the unemployment line.

Which leads us to a perfectly reasonable question: why don't youth football coaches use trick plays more frequently?

Why don't we see a Flea Flicker or a Fake Punt in every single Pop Warner football game? Spare me the argument that the stakes in youth football leagues are still high. No one in Pop Warner is coaching to keep their job and 10 years from now, who will care if the Mr. Tony's Pizza and Grille Red Vikings finished in second place or third? Let's be honest, the primary factor that prevents youth football coaches from adding trick plays into the game plan is the fear of taking risks and failing. Today's youth coaches can be expected to preach to their players about the virtues of being mentally tough and handling failure with their head held high, yet run away as fast as humanly possible from any hint of risk and failure. Anyone else see the irony in that?

The sky today is a brilliant cerulean blue and the geese are honking high overhead. Thick dew covers the carpet of grass at your feet and a touch of frost last night has left a sobering chill in the air this afternoon. You have a mesh bag of footballs slung over your shoulder and two dozen players standing in front of you who have never learned how to properly execute a Fake Double Reverse.

What are you waiting for?

Specialization

If you skim through a Hirschbeck family photo album, one of the first things you notice is that our son is a huge soccer fan. In roughly half of the photos taken of Zac between birth and age 14, there is a soccer ball on his foot or one lying nearby. No one in our family can recall an identifiable time and place where he was introduced to the game, no first soccer team, first goal, or first uniform. Instead, it feels like Zac started to play soccer almost immediately after leaving the womb. From the time he was old enough to walk, he was a soccer player.

Zac started to play travel soccer when he was 10 and over time, he grew to be a pretty talented player. Around the time that he began playing for his middle school team, I started to hear whispers from other parents about tryouts for "premier" teams. I had no idea if Zac was good enough to play on one of those types of teams, but I was intrigued by the idea of watching my son play on a team surrounded by outstanding soccer players.

Quietly, I did some research on teams and leagues that would be a step up from his travel team. The first thing I noticed was that the next step up was very expensive. The total cost of playing travel soccer for a year was roughly $400. Playing on a premier team would cost over $1,500, not including gas money, hotel rooms, and meals while we were on the road.

Playing on a premier team carried a more substantial time commitment than his current team. Zac's travel team practiced in a gym 10 minutes away from our house and played games against clubs that were no more than 30-45 minutes away. A premier team would practice 30 minutes away from our house and play against teams that were 45 minutes to five hours away.

In return for the investment of time, travel, and money, Zac would receive outstanding coaching. He'd be playing with and against the strongest players in our region. Four or five years down the road, he'd play in showcase tournaments attended by college scouts. No one ever made any guarantees, but the implicit message hidden in the literature of every premier club was "if you want your kid to get a college scholarship tomorrow, he or she should be playing on a premier team today."

The lure of a college scholarship was intoxicating. When I briefly attended college back in the early 1980s, the cost was about $600 per semester. My older daughter was looking at schools that had a price tag of $35,000 a year. Frankly, I was feeling unsure of my ability to steer my children to a bright future. For our family, earning a full scholarship to play soccer at a good school was the financial equivalent of winning the lottery.

Though I had no idea where we'd find the time and money to have Zac play on a premier team, I really liked the dream of winning the lottery. Visions of recruiting letters flooding into our mailbox danced in my head. I pictured my hand on his shoulder as he signed his letter of intent and imagined what it might feel like to watch him stride out on to the field for his first game. No one in my family had ever been awarded an athletic scholarship to a Division I school. Everyone would be so proud.

Fortunately, my wife introduced a more sane and reasonable voice to the issue. Tricia pointed out that both of us worked at least 60 hours a week running our own small business. We had a strong marriage, another child besides Zac that we loved dearly, and a variety of hobbies and interests of our own. If we had to start carving out time to travel to Pittsburgh or Cleveland every other weekend for a soccer tournament, it would radically change our life. I love our life the way it is, Tricia said.

So did I. There was a certain balance and symmetry to our life. In contrast to many families, our lives didn't revolve around the kids or one of our jobs. Each of us was given space and support to pursue things that made our heart beat a little faster. Tricia loved to cook and read; Molly was active in school and starting to think about making a living as a writer; I enjoyed training for marathons and getting out in the garden on weekends. If the spotlight was focused almost exclusively on Zac and soccer, it would disrupt our family's equilibrium. Steering $2,000 a year and 20 hours a week toward premier soccer meant that something else would have to give.

Tricia suggested a reasonable compromise: we'd both promise to drop the issue completely until Zac expressed an interest in trying out for a premier team. She noted that if our son really felt passionate about playing soccer at a higher level, Zac would talk to us.

He never did. For the next five years, Zac played at the highest level of travel soccer in our area, but he never expressed an interest in moving beyond that. It wasn't until his junior year of high school that any of us spoke the words 'premier soccer' out loud again. We were on a long car ride to move his sister back home from college after the spring semester.

"Did you ever want me to play premier soccer?" he said.

"I thought about it," I said, "but you never expressed any interest in trying out. Did you want to play?"

"Not really. I thought about it, but it wasn't all that interesting to me."

"Why not?" I asked.

"The guys who played premier were all about soccer, soccer, soccer," he said. "That was the only sport they played during the year. Their whole lives revolved around one sport. I liked playing other sports, too." This was something I never considered when I had researched premier teams years earlier. Zac was more passionate about playing soccer than any other sport, but it wasn't the only game he played. He played baseball, basketball, and ran track for school. If he had played on a premier team, there was no way he could have made a commitment to play on any of those other school teams.

"Do you ever wish you would have played premier just to see how good you could have been?" I asked.

"Sometimes," he said. "I definitely could have been a better player if I had just focused on soccer, but I'm not sure how much better. Maybe I could have played Division I, but probably not." The statistics in our area seemed to support Zac's assessment of his abilities. Thousands of kids played high school sports in our area, but only a few dozen received any type of money to play at a Division I school. "You wanna know what I think would have happened if I had played on a premier team?" Zac asked.

"What?"

"I would have loved it for a year or two—and then I would have hated it. If I had been forced to play soccer 24-7, it would have driven me crazy." He looked at me and looked out the window. "That kind of disappoints you, doesn't it?"

"Absolutely not," I replied. "I'm very proud of you, Zac. Until you have kids of your own, I don't think you'll truly understand how much you and your sister mean to me and your mom."

"But you still kind of wish I would have played on a premier team, don't you?" He wasn't picking a fight; he was just trying to get to the heart of the matter.

"Here's the thing," I said. "As a parent, it's hard for me to shake the idea that we should always push ourselves to be the best we can be. Part of me wonders if you didn't want to play premier soccer because you thought it might have been too hard." The car fell silent for a while. It's not always easy to get to the heart of the matter.

"What's your best marathon time?" he asked.

"A little over 4 hours, 17 minutes. Why?"

"If you really pushed yourself and everything went perfectly, how fast do you think you could run a marathon?"

"I think I could run a 3:30—maybe even a little faster."

"Why don't you?" he asked.

"Why don't I what? Why are we talking about marathons, Zac?"

"Why don't you really push yourself and run a 3:15 marathon?"

"I don't know," I said. "Finishing a marathon was always a goal of mine; running a marathon really fast never was. There are lots of other things that are more important."

"What about the 'pushing ourselves to be the best we can be' thing?" The car fell silent again. I didn't have an answer for him. "Here's what I think," he continued. "Some guys are interested in giving up everything and playing one sport for one team, and some guys are interested in giving up everything and running a 3:15 marathon."

"And then there's us," I said.

"And then there's us," he laughed.

Specializing in one sport at an early age can steer some young athletes onto a path that leads to a Division I scholarship, but it is a path that is filled with significant risk and danger. A child who specializes in one sport places stress on the same joints and muscles 52 weeks a year, which increases the risk of chronic pain and serious injury. Psychological "burn out" is more prevalent in young athletes who play the same sport day after day, week after week, and year after year. If a child devotes almost all of their physical and psychological energy toward the pursuit of one goal, it increases the likelihood that they will grow into a one-dimensional adult, a young man or woman who excels at one or two physical skills and struggles to complete basic scholastic or social tasks.

Despite all of those risks and potential pitfalls, I believe that all young athletes should be allowed to chase the holy grail of a college scholarship—even if it means specializing. If a 12-year-old kid is obsessed with the idea of playing shooting guard for Duke someday and truly loves playing basketball and nothing but basketball, what gives us the right to stomp all over his dreams? Just as it is possible for a 48-year-old guy to run 3:15 marathon, it is possible for an 18-year-old guy to play Division I sports, earn a 3.5 GPA, and develop a variety of hobbies and interests all at the same time. The idea that all specialization is inherently harmful to children makes for a nice urban legend, but the truth is specialization works sometimes.

The keys to deciding if specializing might be a good idea for your child lie in three basic questions:

Does my child possess the physical tools to play one sport at a high level of competition? If a child does not have the athleticism and ability to play at a high level, the other two questions are irrelevant.

Is this my child's dream? Problems related to specialization can usually be traced to parents who try to force their own dreams for their child onto their son or daughter. Young athletes are much more likely to grow miserable pursuing a goal if the goal wasn't theirs in the first place.

Will the sacrifices needed to specialize in one sport compromise the structure of our family? Looking back, I'm not convinced our family would have worked if it had been built around premier soccer. Some families can sacrifice the time and money needed to specialize, some can't.

Stupid

I have a friend who was heavily involved in drugs when she attended college. Among other transgressions, she was kicked out of school twice and spent a few days in jail down in Florida. In her mid-twenties, she turned her life around. She quit drugs completely, went back to school, met a really good guy at an internship, got her degree, and married the same really good guy two years later. Nineteen years down the road, they have two beautiful girls and still appear to be madly in love with each other.

Her story is a slightly skewed embodiment of the modern day American dream. Girl snorts a pile of coke, girl gets arrested, girl courageously gets sober and meets the love of her life, and girl builds a warm and loving family.

To date, her 15- and 18-year-old daughters have never heard that story. They believe that their mom never smoked, never drank until she was 18, and never kissed a guy until she met their dad. From the beginning, my friend has changed facts and omitted huge chunks of narrative when talking to her daughters about her life. If she tells her daughters the unblemished truth about her first 22 years on the planet, she believes that her daughters won't respect her anymore. How can I forbid the girls from picking up a cigarette, she wonders, if they know I spent a weekend in a Miami Dade jail cell?

Though I've never done time in the slammer, I have had a longtime love affair with Stupidity. We first eyed each other from across a crowded room at a party I attended on the night that I graduated from high school. For 17 years, I was a well-behaved young man who always played by the rules. Stupidity told me that my reward for being a good boy all those years was to finally allow myself a taste of the wild side. In four hours, I drank half of a bottle of vodka all by myself. My blood alcohol content must have been at least .20 at the time—probably higher.

My friend's parents were out of town and it had been decided well beforehand that we'd all crash there for the night. It seemed like a safe and sensible plan. No DWIs, no curfews to be met, and no recriminations from our parents. We'd drink and puke until the sun came up, pass out on the carpet, and hang out at my friend's until we got reasonably sober. It seemed like a romantic, swashbuckling way to graduate from high school.

Stupidity thought that was a foolish plan. She sat on my lap, looked deep into my eyes, and convinced me that only wimps who couldn't hold their liquor crashed on the carpet. Men went home. So shortly after guzzling my last mouthful of vodka for the evening and falling into a bed of tomato plants, I went home.

Thankfully, I wasn't dumb enough to get behind the wheel of a car, but I did feel confident enough to try to ride my friend's bike home. My confidence was misplaced. Roughly two hundred yards from my front door, I blacked out. One minute I was riding down Crosby Avenue singing Bruce Springsteen songs at the top of my lungs, and the next minute I was lying in the middle of the street, the ride side of my face covered in blood and the front wheel of the bike folded over like a taco shell.

Fortunately, my tale has a happy ending. No ambulances, IVs or overnight stays in the hospital. Just a slight concussion, a massive brush burn that covered half of my face, and the humiliation of having to stumble home and face my family. Yet I often look back on that night and think about what might have been. Under slightly different circumstances, I could have been seriously injured. If I had blacked out a few seconds earlier or later, I could have easily wound up dead.

As soon as the first whiff of drugs and alcohol entered the lives of our two kids, I sat them down and told them what they now refer to as The Vodka Story. The first time both of them heard it, their jaws unhinged from their skulls. My daughter had tears in her eyes. It was shocking for Molly and Zac to imagine an alternate universe in which their father is happily riding a bike into a busy intersection at 2 a.m. while singing an impassioned version of "Thunder Road" and then, seconds later, he's a dead mass of twisted limbs and blood under the fender of an Oldsmobile Cutlass.

During their formative years, most children view their parents as superheroes. Even after they learn the truth, most kids cling to the narrow worldview that mom and dad are a few mistakes away from infallible. Looking back, it wasn't just violent imagery that made The Vodka Story a profound experience for my kids, it was the recognition that their father had the capacity to make enormously reckless and stupid decisions.

To date, there has not been a single DWI, blackout, or alcohol-fueled act of stupidity among my friend's daughters or our two kids. I'd bet good money on the fact that all four kids have dipped their toes into .05 to .10 territory, but they have done so in safe environments surrounded by friends they can trust. My friend and I have taken very different routes in educating our kids about substance abuse, but all four of our kids have adopted the same responsible attitudes towards drugs and alcohol. Chalk it up as one more piece of evidence supporting the belief that there is more than one way to raise a child.

However, there is one significant difference between my friend's route and mine. I have told my children the truth while my friend has looked her kids in the eye and lied to them. My friend carries around the weight of worrying about how her kids will react when the finally learn the truth. When my head hits the pillow at the end of the day, I sleep soundly.

For me, trust is an essential part of establishing a positive relationship with a teenager and last time I checked, trust is a two-way street. If my daughter arrives home an hour after curfew, I must be able to trust that her excuse is honest and valid. If that same daughter asks me if I've ever gotten drunk and done something really stupid, she must be able to trust that I will tell her the truth. How can we expect our kids to tell us the unblemished truth if we feed them a strict diet of fairytales and fables?

I'm Losing You

Last week, I heard from a friend who has decided to separate from his wife. He's been married 15 years and has three beautiful kids. It's a sad story that my wife and I hear a lot these days and I get the feeling that there are more stories on the horizon. In bed last night, Tricia and I counted seven friends who have separated or divorced over the past 18 months.

Each of those seven stories is different, but each contains at least one common thread. In each marriage, there was a man or woman who became infatuated with their kids while they gradually grew indifferent to their spouse. Soccer tournaments grew more important than going out to dinner and holding hands during dessert. PTA meetings took priority over cuddling on the couch and watching a good movie.

If you tossed a little truth serum in her morning tea, I think my wife would admit that our children are generally a lot more lovable and fascinating than I am. Our kids come home each day with open hearts and stories to tell. Our son makes us laugh every day and even at the age of 20, our daughter still speaks in hyper, swirling sentences that contain no commas or periods. Each of the kid's days seems more interesting than the day that came before.

Each of my days seems very similar to the one that came before. The number of cute and funny things I say on a yearly basis is roughly equal to the number of times I flex my abs on the cover of *Men's Health* magazine. I come home from work and soak my feet in ice so

I'll be able to walk the next day. I wear pairs of soccer shorts that are older than my 15-year-old son.

Yet when it comes to matters relating to love and marriage, change is highly overrated, isn't it? Back in 1983, I fell in love with my wife because she was funny, confident, and had the most beautiful eyes of any woman I'd ever met. Today, I love her for lots of reasons, but the most obvious are that she is funny, confident, and still has the most beautiful eyes of any woman I've ever met. She's changed a lot over the years, but when it comes to those things that are most important to me, she's still the same woman she was 25 years ago.

I'd venture a guess that Tricia still hangs out with me for the same reasons. Set aside the icepacks, cantankerous disposition, and 17-year-old soccer shorts and I'm still the guy who is partially responsible for a lot of the things that she holds most dear in her life.

It has been said that the most important gift that a parent can give to a child is a good marriage. The older I get, the more I think that's true. Our daughter doesn't need me to select her college courses for her, but she does need me to show her how a husband treats his wife. Our son doesn't need Tricia to step in and deal with an obnoxious coach at school, but he definitely needs to see how she deals with an occasionally obnoxious husband at home.

Back in the early 1970s, my generation of parents became consumed with making our kids happy. Children, not marriage, became the focal point of many families. Right around the same time, the divorce rate in our country spiked into the 40 percent range and has remained at that level ever since. Am I the only guy that sees a correlation between those two trends?

Seems to me like the writing is on the wall. If you spend your 20s and 30s hovering over your child and ignoring your spouse, it increases the likelihood that you'll spend part of your 40s or 50s in divorce court.

Our Work Here Is Done

I am writing this out in the backyard on our youngest child's 18th birthday. All things considered, it's better for me to be outside weeping over my keyboard than inside weeping onto my son's birthday cake.

Actually, not a single tear has been shed as we push our last kid toward the door. Since Zac's high school graduation, the prevailing emotion swirling around in my head has been relief. It feels like most of the heavy lifting associated with raising kids is over. Our children have morphed into two smart, funny, respectful, and humble adults. I'm not exactly sure how that happened, but it did.

Lately, I've been thinking about what I've learned over the past 23 years. I'm a very different dad than I was back in 1986. Back then, most of my parenting decisions were only slightly less questionable than my wardrobe choices. Here are several things I know now that I wish I knew then:

The Best Gift a Parent Can Give To a Child Is a Strong Marriage

Over the past 25 years, Tricia and I have gone through a few periods where we've lost each other. Those dark periods never lasted more than a month or two, and they always related to our kids. Usually, we became so immersed in being there for our kids that we forgot to be there for each other.

A healthy marriage teaches children essential messages about love, family, communication, respect, problem solving, and dozens of other life skills. Protect your marriage at all costs, even if it means saying "no" to dance classes or travel hockey for your kids.

When Placed Under Stress, We Forget What We Know

A 10-year-old soccer player possesses outstanding skills, but in the final minutes of a close game, he starts to hack at the ball instead of possess it. Why? Because when placed in a stressful environment, the 10-year-old forgets what he knows. Stress often makes us forget who we are and what we know to be true.

Like most parents, Tricia and I have experienced more than a few stressful situations. One of our kids has a fairly serious chronic illness, we run our own business, and Tricia drives like a maniac. When forced to handle adversity, we always try to remember who we are and what we're capable of.

Teach From the Good

One of the most gifted soccer coaches I've ever met possessed a unique ability to teach from a positive perspective at all times. Instead of barking "I've never seen us pass this poorly" he'd say "The best passer on the field today is Jenna; here is why she's successful." There is a subtle but important distinction between those two messages.

Many parents teach from the bad. They wait for their child to make mistakes and reprimand them. It is just as important to identify and support a child's good decisions as it is to correct bad behavior.

Pick Your Spots

It's natural for parents to obsess over their kids, but sometimes the object of our obsession is pretty strange. I've met moms and dads who are completely consumed with their child's hair, batting stance, or relationships. When my daughter brought home her first boyfriend, I couldn't stop thinking about the little punk.

We have three basic rules in our family: we treat each other with love and respect; we give an honest effort in everything we do; we adopt realistic and responsible attitudes towards sex and drugs. With the exception of the first boyfriend, I've tried to ignore all the silly stuff and focus on those three rules.

Encourage Your Child To Make Their Own Decisions

In a past life, I ran a large summer camp. It was our policy to encourage our campers to make responsible decisions. If campers asked for permission to do something that didn't impact their safety, our response was always nine powerful words: "Whatever you decide to do is fine with me."

Tricia and I have a great deal of trust in our children. That trust was forged when our kids were five years old. When they asked if they should color Donald Duck yellow or wear their shirts backwards, whatever they decided was fine with us.

Don't Be Afraid To Make Discipline Memorable

When our daughter was five, she went through an obnoxious stage when she thought she was entitled to a new Barbie every week. Tricia and I quickly realized it was time to stop the free flow of Barbies into our daughter's hot little hands.

After dealing with half a dozen tantrums, I tossed Molly into her car seat and took her for a drive over to the East Side of Buffalo, a section of the city filled with violence and crime. Her jaw unhinged and her eyes grew as wide as saucers when she entered this foreign land, a world in which young girls didn't count the number of Barbies they had in their toy chest. Almost 20 years later, Molly refers to that trip to as one of the best things we ever did for her.

The Best Help Is Usually In Your Backyard

At last count, there were 273,988,041 books on parenting at your local bookstore. I suppose some of those books have value, but it never made much sense to me to search for parenting advice in books. Dr. Phil, Dr. Laura, and Dr. Spock all share three common traits: they don't know my kids, they don't know me, and they are much more interested in selling me their book than helping me be a better dad.

Over the past 23 years, there have been several times when I felt completely unqualified to be a dad. When I was struggling, the most effective thing I could do was look at moms and dads that I believed were great parents, and model my behavior after them.

Tell Your Kids How You Feel

My mom was one of the most generous, loving people I've ever met, but it wasn't until later in her life that she felt comfortable saying the words "I love you" out loud. I think it was the birth of her grandchildren that turned mom into a hugger and unleashed hundreds of I love yous to those closest to her.

Shortly after my kids were born, I decided that I didn't want to wait until I was 60 to start telling my kids I loved them. It's rare that day passes without everyone in our home saying those three words out loud.

Walk Away Little Girl

In a matter of weeks, our daughter, Molly, will be moving out of town to take a job as a television producer in Albany, New York. It is impossible for her to contain her excitement these days. She'll be in the center of the New York State political scene, she loves the staff and structure at her new station, and she has found a really nice apartment five minutes away from work.

I make no claims to objectivity when it comes to evaluating my child's abilities, but it appears as though our kid has her personal and professional stuff together. In a short period of time, she has built a strong reputation within her profession and on top of that, she has dated a really good guy for several years. She is a talented young woman in a stable relationship with a young man that I genuinely like and respect. Who could ask for anything more?

Actually, I have several requests. First, I'd like Mr. Jim Bell, the executive producer of *The Today Show*, to call my daughter tomorrow and offer her a job as an assistant producer. Second, I'd like Molly to inform Mr. Jim Bell that while she'd love to accept the position, she has serious concerns about relocating to New York City. Third, I'd like Mr. Jim Bell to wave his hand dismissively and say, "No problem, Molly. I've heard such great things about your producing skills that there is no need for you to relocate. We'll need you to travel to the big stuff like presidential inaugurations, the Olympics, or an appearance by Bruce Springsteen and the E Street Band on *The Today Summer Concert Series sponsored by Toyota*, but 90 percent of the time you can work from home right there in beautiful and bucolic

Buffalo, NY." Fourth, I'd like Molly to accept the position and inform the good folks at News 9 in Albany that Mr. Jim Bell made her an offer she couldn't refuse. Finally, I'd like Molly to purchase a center entrance colonial in North Buffalo with a bay window and a big oak mantel onto which she can place all of the Emmys, Pulitzers, and National Press Club awards that she'll be raking in over the next few decades.

Though Mr. Jim Bell hasn't returned my phone calls yet, I'm hopeful that we can collaborate to construct a scenario that works for all of us. Mr. Jim Bell gets to add a gifted young journalist to the staff of America's highest-rated morning news program, Molly gets a job that any young journalist would kill to have, and I get to see my little girl whenever I want.

Before anyone suggests that these requests might be a little unreasonable, I should note that almost everything I'm asking for here is negotiable. For example, I'm not locked in to *The Today Show* or NBC. If an executive producer on a highly regarded news show on CBS, ABC, or CNN is interested in offering Molly a job, I'm listening. The key point here is to keep Molly in Buffalo. I want the beautiful young woman who makes my heart feel a little lighter every time I hear her laugh right here where I can see her. Four and a half hours away by car, five hours and 22 minutes by train, or even one hour and 15 minutes by US Airways Flight #4751 simply will not do.

This is all kind of pitiful, isn't it? Our kid is in a wonderful place in her life right now. She's taking risks in the pursuit of her dreams and here I am dancing around the outer edge of a full-scale nervous breakdown.

I am not alone. Recently, my wife and I have started playing an unusual game that I call "What'll Happen If?" The rules of the game are pretty simple. I'll be sound asleep at 3:00 a.m. and Tricia will grab my shoulder and whisper, "What'll happen if Molly gets really sick and passes out on the floor of her apartment?"

"Don't worry, honey," I'll mumble. "Her roommate would find her and get her to a doctor. If she was really sick, we'd drop everything and go take care of her."

We're eating breakfast the next morning and it's my turn. "What'll happen," I ask, "if Molly is out at a bar with friends from work and some sleazy guy slips something in her drink and tries to take advantage of her?" Tricia pets our dog, Lily, and frowns. This is a tough one.

"First of all, Molly isn't the type to hang around in bars all night. Second, I'm sure her girlfriends wouldn't let her take off with some weird, sleazy guy. Third, if some guy ever did try to take advantage of Molly, you'd hunt him down like an animal and kill him with your bare hands."

My wife knows me well—much better than I know myself. Tricia has always told me that I'd be a puddling mass of tears and tissues if one of the kids ever moved out of town, but I've always thought I'd be able to handle the transition pretty well. I pictured myself as the Shoulder To Cry On, the pillar of strength that gives my wife a consoling hug as I plan the conversion of the newly abandoned bedroom into my home office. As departure day draws closer, I realize that my wife was right all along. On the way home from getting Molly settled in Albany, Tricia will be the one figuring out how to maintain a close and loving relationship with our daughter from a distance of 284 miles. I'll be the one wailing like a schoolgirl as we pull through the Williamsville tollbooths.

My anticipated collapse into the fetal position doesn't separate me from most guys I know. Women are superior to men in managing the transition into the second half of their lives. Menopause is no walk in the park, but it is a gradual process, an inevitable transformation that every woman knows awaits them from the time they step out of high school health class.

A man's introduction to the second half of their life is usually stark and brutal. During a game of pick-up basketball with the guys, our sciatic nerve swoops out of the trees and eats our face off. After bed rest and medication, we recover a reduced percentage of our strength and dignity, but there is always the subconscious recognition that our sciatic nerve can pay us a return visit whenever it likes. Soon, we realize that our sciatic nerve is not a loner. It has friends. Turns out our sex drive and our sciatic nerve dated the same girls in high school.

Our sciatic nerve and our ability to stay awake past 9:30 p.m. played on the same Little League baseball team. Rumors circulate that three dozen friends attended our sciatic nerve's birthday party and we wonder who else will pop into our lives and shred our masculinity when we least expect it.

In my high school health class, there was plenty of information on making babies and even more information on not making babies, but no one ever talked about the day when our firstborn baby wouldn't be around much anymore. The cold realization that life will contain a little less light and a little more loneliness has hit me hard. I have never thought much about a place and time where our kids are alive and my wife and I are not, but I do now. Leaving my kids just as my mother and father have left me is a thought so sad that I cannot entertain it for very long. Beautiful day out today, isn't it? What's for dinner tonight?

A few weeks ago on Christmas Eve, there was a beautiful full moon hanging low over the horizon and it led me to wonder how many Christmas Eves there are in my future. Maybe 20? Thirty-five if I'm really lucky? If there is a bright side to my daughter leaving town and my corresponding newfound mortality, it is the recognition that everything that I hold close to my heart in the weeks and months and years ahead is finite. The trick to growing old gracefully, I think, is to appreciate the day without feeling compelled to squeeze every ounce of oxygen from every single moment. In the second half of a parent's life, our job is to be there for our kids and make sure they know how much they are loved. The rest is up to them.

Of course, all bets are off if a grandchild enters the picture. If Molly places a smiling baby in my arms, there will be no room for growing old gracefully. Albany, here we come.

Made in United States
North Haven, CT
07 August 2023

40057448R00111